Whispers from My Heart

Whispers from My Heart

— LEARNING TO QUIET THE NOISE —

Tony Garcia

ISBN-13: 9781979496919
ISBN-10: 1979496919
Library of Congress Control Number: 2017917409
CreateSpace Independent Publishing Platform
North Charleston, South Carolina

For my mom:
For your loving heart.
For your gentle whispers I have heard throughout my life.

Preface

Four years ago, I made the decision to try and qualify for the Boston Marathon. At the time, I had no reason to believe that qualifying was within the realm of possibility. I had only three marathons to my credit, all of which I ran in over or near four hours. Plus, I was such a novice, I didn't even know what my Boston qualifying time was. I was comfortably sliding into my fifties, with few challenges in my life, seemingly little left to chase. What made me believe I would ever stand at the starting line of the Boston Marathon? I am not sure I have come to terms with that answer yet. I simply felt it was a dream I needed to chase down. Something about it called my name.

As I began my journey, I began recording my struggles, setbacks, minor victories, random musings, life chats, secrets, truths, and whispers. The response from others was often, "This applies to life as well as running." The more I wrote, the more it became clear I wasn't writing about running at all. I, indeed, was writing about life and living. I was merely using running as an analogy for the life I wanted to live, to capture all I was searching for in my life.

All the miles I traveled encompassed my personal journey toward a dream—one not tied to a run, but one for my life. A dream I hold in my heart. A dream that simply whispered to me.

And as I learned to quiet the noise, I began to understand my journey, my failures, my struggles, myself on an entirely new level. What follows in these pages are lessons, letters, poems, stories, and quiet reminders of the miles I have traveled.

Miles of constant doubt, yet miles of knowing my ultimate truth. Miles filled with fear, yet miles filled with a courage I had never known.

Miles wondering, "Am I worthy?" yet miles believing, "I always have been." Miles lost along a broken road, yet miles leading me home.

Miles too difficult to bear, yet miles overcoming my own impossible. Miles knowing only breathlessness and brokenness, yet miles finally allowing me to breathe and heal.

Miles of pure anguish, yet miles of sheer *holiness*.

I continue to write. I continue to run. I continue to chase the dreams set before my life. I continue to listen to the whispers from my heart, knowing, as I simply continue to move forward, that all my truths, answers, and dreams will come to be.

And as you read the words found scribbled across these pages, I hope they quietly whisper of hopes and light and faith and love. I hope they speak directly to your heart.

This is a whisper from my heart.

—G

January 1

We will open the book. Its pages are blank. We are going to put words on them ourselves. The book is called Opportunity and its first chapter is New Year's Day.
—Edith Lovejoy Pierce

Dear New Year,

There are some things I need you to know about me before you welcome me in.

I am not in a hurry. Please do not rush me through your days and months. Be patient with me. Do not push me forward, for I am moving at the pace I need, for me. Allow me time to make mistakes, to explore, to get lost, to simply rest, to simply be. Learning takes time. I am still learning. Growing requires time. I am still growing. This is my time.

I am not asking for easy. I know you might be filled with difficulties and obstacles. That is nothing new. The years before you presented their own challenges. I am strong enough to face what you have in store. What I ask is that you play fair. And don't give me "Life isn't fair." Life has rules: be kind, do no harm, tell the truth. Play by the rules. This is my request.

I am not who I once was. You are aware of my history. It walked me to your doorstep. And yet, it does not define me. I am allowed to change. I am allowed to find and walk and follow a new path. I am allowed to decide yesterday's answers are no longer true. I am allowed to dream different dreams, chase different rainbows. This is my right.

I am not afraid of the unknown. I do not know of your plans. I do not know what you hold. But I am not frightened. For I believe. I believe in beauty and peace. I believe in miracles and hope. I believe in goodness and truth. I believe in light and love. If you do not hold such things, you too shall pass. And I will be okay. This is my courage.

I am not always sure of where I am going, of what I need or want, of who I am. And thus, I constantly am searching: For a place to finally call home. For a sense of fulfillment. For immutable truths. For an unwavering love. I have seen such things, felt them ever so close to my heart. I know they exist. Of that I am sure. This is my journey.

Now you know a little about me. I look forward to meeting you, spending time with you. Let's make it a good one.

Love,

Me

January 2

Affirmations are our mental vitamins, providing the
supplementary positive thoughts we need to balance the barrage
of negative events and thoughts we experience daily.
—*Tia Walker*

These are my affirmations.

Dear Life,

I wonder if you know.

I wonder if you know how brave I am.
Despite the doubts, fears, and worries, I have the courage to walk through your darkness.
I am brave.

I wonder if you know how strong I am.
Despite the weakness, falls, and failures, I summon the strength to rise every single time.
I am strong.

I wonder if you know how special I am.
Despite the loss, heartache, and pain, I find a way to simply forgive.
I am special.

I wonder if you know how worthy I am.
Despite the past, the mistakes, and the wrongs done me, I have remained ever giving.
I am worthy.

I wonder if you know how amazing I am.
Despite the broken promises, broken dreams, and broken road, I remain hope-filled.
I am amazing.

I wonder if you know how beautiful I am.
Despite the scars, wrinkles, and tiredness etched upon me, I possess a loving heart, a gentle spirit, a radiant light.
I am beautiful.

Brave. Strong. Special. Worthy. Amazing. Beautiful. This—this is who I am.

I wonder if you know.

Love,

Me

January 3

I am not what you see. I am what time and effort and interaction slowly unveil.
—Richelle E. Goodrich

Dear Life,

If you think I will be broken,
You must not know me,
For I am unbreakable.

If you think I will surrender,
You must not know me,
For I am a warrior.

If you think I will stop believing,
You must not know me,
For I am a true believer.

If you think I will let go of hope,
You must not know me,
For I am hope-filled.

If you think I will succumb to darkness,
You must not know me,
For I am a light.

If you think I will stand in fear,
You must not know me,
For I am courage.

If you think I will give up on love,
You must not know me,
For I am unwavering.

If you think I will be anything less,
You must not know me,
For I am me.

Love,

Me

January 4

I was on the path of the warrior, when I realized I was the warrior.
—Neetal Parekh

I am strong.
Enough to rise again.

I am strong.
Enough to overcome.

I am strong.
Enough to hope.

I am strong.
Enough to believe.

I am strong.
Enough to lift another.

I am strong.
Enough.

I am quick.
To forgive.

I am quick.
To listen.

I am quick.
To offer a hand.

I am quick.
To seek peace.

I am quick.
To dream.

I am quick.
To love.

Strength and quickness.

These. These are the markings of a warrior.

January 5

*When witnessing to those closest to us sometimes the only way
we can get through to them is to set an example.*
—Amanda Penland

Dear You,

I reflected on what I witnessed about you, and I wanted to sit and write you a letter. Have you stopped recently to appreciate how truly remarkable you are? To fully embrace just how special and amazing you are? I am learning lessons about you, and they humble me.

I witnessed as you pushed your body to new limits, to new places, beyond your threshold, and I marveled. Despite all the things you do not like about your body, your perceived imperfections and flaws, your wishing you could make it different, it is capable of producing miracles. Your body is a remarkable work of art, a thing of beauty, an incredible machine. Embrace it, talk gently to it, and learn to truly love it.

I witnessed as you pushed through trials and pain, setbacks and heartache, and I am amazed by your spirit and strength. Despite the odds and difficulties, challenges and obstacles, you refuse to quit. You continue to rise and try again. Your spirit is powerful beyond measure. You are stronger than you know. Give yourself credit, breathe deep, and begin again; it is what you know to do.

I witnessed as you shone your light on others, and I basked in its brilliant glow. You are a gift, a wonder in the world; you make a difference, and you change lives. Do not shy away from your own light. Acknowledge how special you are; let that light shine on yourself so you can see all the beauty and wonder that we see in you.

I witnessed as you continued to chase your dreams, as you set new goals, as you pursued the horizon, and I am inspired. Don't ever give up on your dreams. Have faith, keep hope, walk toward these dreams every day, know they are achievable. You inspire so many, you give hope to others, you help us reach our dreams.

You are beautiful, strong, a brilliant light, a keeper of dreams. You are a very special gift. When you gently unfold, we are all rewarded.

May you walk this day knowing how truly remarkable and special you are.

I have been a witness, and I know.

Love,

Me

January 6

Maybe it's time for the fighter to be fought for, the holder
to be held, and for the lover to be loved.
—Unknown

Dear Life,

I fought for you: Fought fears both real and imagined. Fought demons that haunt your waking and your dreams. Fought a past that cannot be erased.

I fought for you—as a fighter does, unwaveringly. Maybe it's time you fought for me.

I was there to hold you: There to hold you in the depths of your darkness. There to hold you close enough to feel your brokenness. There to hold you in an embrace safe and warm.

I was there to hold you—as a holder does, unwaveringly. Maybe it's time you were there to hold me.

I loved you: Loved you when you believed you were not worthy of love. Loved you when you were at your worst. Loved you enough to forgive you.

I loved you—as a lover does, unwaveringly. Maybe it's time you loved me.

Maybe it's time.

Love,

Me

January 7

Advice to my younger self: Start where you are with what you have, try
not to hurt other people, take more chances, if you fail, keep trying.
—Germany Kent

This is an open letter to my five-year-old self.

Dear Little One,

You do not know what this life will hold, my sweet child. So much to learn, so much awaits you, so much you shall experience. If you could hear my words, these are the things I wish I could say to you: Fear less. So much you will learn to fear will never happen. Fear less. It will steal so much from you. Fear less. Especially in matters of the heart. Trust. Faith. Love.

Listen. With intention. Without judgment. Others have a story; you can learn much from them. Listen. Before rushing to speak. More than you speak. Listen. To understand. To build trust, friendships, bridges. Speak your truth, always. Use your words to help, to heal, to forgive. Speak your truth, gently. Use your words for peace, for good, for love. Speak your truth, quietly. To be heard, you need not be the loudest voice in the room, but you must have something of value to say.

Do not confuse popularity with respect. Strive to be respected. Do not confuse possessions with worth. You are priceless, not a price tag. Do not confuse weakness with humility. There is much strength in quietly believing in yourself. Do your math. Count your blessings more than your problems. Kindness counts. Do your math. Subtract yourself from negative situations and negative people. Do not reduce or minimize the worth of another. Do your math. Add value. Multiply joy.

Collect more memories than more things. Life is made, not bought. Collect yourself in times of stress and sorrow. You are made to handle these. Collect the fleeting. Rainbows and goose bumps and moments of breathlessness. Remember. Say "please" and "thank you." They always matter. Remember. Where you came from, who you are, what you believe in. These should always guide you. Remember. You are worthy of love. This is always the truth.

Feel free. To make mistakes, to try again, to change your mind. Be free. Enough to dance, enough to sing, enough to laugh. Live free. Of prejudice, of hatred, of violence. Live life as an action verb. Think. Read. Learn. Do. Live life as an action verb. Give. Serve. Help. Love. Live life as an action verb. Soar. Believe. Hope. Dream.

There is so much more to share with you, sweet child. But much you must find out for yourself. This life will pass all too quickly. Live it fully. Love it completely. With all your heart.

Now go, little one. Time to be on your way. You have so much to do. I will be waiting for you.

Love, Me

January 8

It takes strength and courage to admit the truth.
—Rick Riordan

I said, "I forgive you." And my voice trembled.
For I feared I would be hurt again.

I said, "I want you." And my voice hesitated.
For I feared I would not be worthy.

I said, "I miss you." And my voice broke.
For I feared I no longer crossed your mind.

I said, "I am sorry." And my voice shook.
For I feared I would not be forgiven.

I said, "I need help." And my voice trailed off.
For I feared I would be seen as weak.

I said, "I am afraid." And my voice cracked.
For I feared I would never find the courage.

I said, "I love you." And my voice quivered.
For I feared I would be met with silence.

I spoke all the truths of my heart. And my voice, how it did shake.
But my heart finally found its rhythm.

January 9

You will go on and meet someone else and I'll just be a chapter in your tale,
but for me, you were, you are and you always will be, the whole story.
—Marian Keyes

Dear Life,

So much has changed. As you are oft to do.
And yet one truth remains. I am still so in love with you.

When times come so hard, I recall moments of such sweet surrender.
And I fall in love with you again.

When the fall comes, I recall moments of being lifted by your grace.
And I fall in love with you again.

When nights come so cold and empty, I recall days wrapped in your warm embrace.
And I fall in love with you again.

When the tears come, I recall moments of pure, unbridled joy.
And I fall in love with you again.

When ugly truths come, I recall moments captivated by your unimaginable beauty.
And I fall in love with you again.

When the doubt comes, I recall moments of believing so deeply in you.
And I fall in love with you again.

When burdens come so heavy, I recall moments of knowing that love bears all.
And I fall in love with you again.

When time with you comes to an end, one truth remains.
I will still be so in love with you.

Love,

Me

January 10

Formerly, when I would feel a desire to understand someone, or myself, I would take into consideration not actions, in which everything is relative, but wishes. Tell me what you want and I'll tell you who you are.
—Anton Chekhov

This. This is my wish for you.

Should shadows appear, may it be because the sun shines upon you.

A light to always guide you home.

Peace. Of mind. Peace. In your heart.

The ability to forgive. Yourself.

Quiet and clarity. To hear your truth. To live it.

A nook. To gently rest your head, your weary, your heart.

An embrace from which you do not want to let go.

Freedom. From the chains which bind you.

Hope. Always hope.

A strength. To keep you from your knees.

That you may come to know the awe and wonder of you.

A life as amazing and beautiful as you.

Love unwavering and true.

A someone who wishes all this for you.

This. My wish. For you.

January 11

He explained to me with great insistence that every question
possessed a power that did not lie in the answer.
—Elie Wiesel

Life has questions. I have answers. This is another life chat.

Life: How will you handle the very worst I have to offer?
Me: By giving you the very best I have to give.

Life: What will you do when my storms rage?
Me: I will become a safe harbor.

Life: When my darkness arrives, how shall you face it?
Me: With a light that cannot be dimmed.

Life: Should I try to break you, how will you respond?
Me: By being gentle enough to bend, yet too strong to break.

Life: What if I do wrong against you?
Me: You will be met with forgiveness.

Life: Will you love me when I seem most unreasonable and unlovable?
Me: It is then that I shall love you most. Unconditionally. Unwaveringly.

Life: How can you do all of this for me, when I've done all of this to you?
Me: It is simple. This is how I want to live.

January 12

Forgiveness is the fragrance that the violet sheds on the heel that has crushed it.
—Mark Twain

This is a letter of forgiveness. To myself.

Dear Me,

I am sorry for the wrongs I have committed against you. You never deserved to be treated like this.

I am sorry for being embarrassed by you. For believing you are not beautiful. For believing you are not worthy of the light. For believing your gifts should never be spoken of.

I am sorry for blaming you. For that which you were not responsible for. For that which you could not control. For the hurtful actions of others.

I am sorry for allowing others to make you feel unworthy. Unworthy of their time. Unworthy of their attention. Unworthy of their love.

I am sorry for not standing up for you. For letting you be viewed as an option. For permitting your dignity to be stolen. For making you feel you are not good enough.

I am sorry for making you bow. To the whims and wishes of others. To the fears and doubts of others. To the untruths of others.

I am sorry for apologizing. For your gentle and kind ways. For your ability to give unconditionally. For the unwavering love you have to offer.

I am sorry. You never deserved to be treated like this.

You were, and always have been, deserving only of love.

Love,

Me

January 13

Did I offer peace today? Did I bring a smile to someone's face? Did I say
words of healing? Did I let go of my anger and resentment? Did I forgive? Did
I love? These are the real questions. I must trust that the little bit of love that
I sow now will bear many fruits, here in this world and the life to come.
—Henri Nouwen

I offer my hand and my heart.
Gently.
In hopes you know peace.

I offer my smile and kindness.
Gently.
In hopes you find your smile.

I offer my prayers and thoughts.
Gently.
In hopes you begin to heal.

I offer to put down my weapons of hurt.
Gently.
In hopes you know we are not at war.

I offer my forgiveness.
Gently.
In hopes you begin to forgive yourself.

I offer my unwavering love.
Gently.
In hopes you will feel it again in your heart.

The questions I face each day do not worry me.

For if you know me, you already know my answers.

January 14

Light thinks it travels faster than anything but it is wrong. No matter how fast light travels, it finds the darkness has always got there first, and is waiting for it.
—Terry Pratchett

Dear Friend,

Light preceded the darkness.

And by the very nature of things, it must also return to follow it.

Peace preceded the chaos.

And by the very nature of things, it must also return to follow it.

Faith preceded the doubt.

And by the very nature of things, it must also return to follow it.

Strength preceded the weakness.

And by the very nature of things, it must also return to follow it.

Hope preceded the despair.

And by the very nature of things, it must also return to follow it.

Love preceded the emptiness.

And by the very nature of things, it must also return to follow it.

I wish you light, peace, faith, strength, hope, and love.

Knowing, by the very nature of things, they will return.

Love,

Me

January 15

If nothing else in this long and short life, let me be true to my conscience,
to the dignity of my own heart. Let me act in a way that says, I have
honored my spirit as truly as I have honored others'. Let me stand
tall and rooted as a mountain in the face of a quaking world.
—Jennifer DeLucy

When your world is quaking,
The ground unsteady,
May hope be your anchor.

When your world is quaking,
Fear settling in,
May faith calm your anxious.

When your world is quaking,
Been driven to your knees,
May honor of self help you rise once more.

When your world is quaking,
The rumbling so loud,
May the quiet bring your answers.

When your world is quaking,
All roads seemingly broken,
May the truth of your conscience lead you home.

When your world is quaking,
A pounding in your chest,
May dignity be held in your heart.

When your world is quaking,
The brokenness so real,
May knowing someone will gently hold your pieces, help you heal.

When your world is quaking,
Your life so very shaken,
May an unwavering love finally stop your trembling.

January 16

The moon does not fight. It attacks no one. It does not worry. It does not
try to crush others. It keeps to its course, but by its very nature, it gently
influences. What other body could pull an entire ocean from shore to shore?
The moon is faithful to its nature and its power is never diminished.
—Ming-Dao Deng

If I came only to illuminate the darkness,
Would you simply accept my light?

If I came quietly to your shores,
Would you rest in my calmness?

If I came gently unto you,
Would you open your arms to embrace me?

If I came softly into your world,
Would you welcome me home?

If I came to see you safely through to the new dawn,
Would you not let me go?

I will rise again tomorrow.
For you. Simply look up.

And, I will remain faithful to my nature.
A light. Quiet. Gentle. Humble. Kind.

January 17

The thing about knowing you're broken is that knowing is not enough to fix it.
—John Goode

Knowing is not enough.
You must do something.
Something new.
Something beyond your comfort.
Something courageous.

Knowing is not enough.
You must want different.
A different path.
A different story.
A different ending.

Knowing is not enough.
You must make a choice.
Choose healthy.
Choose to get off your knees.
Choose to fight for it.

Knowing is not enough.
You must make changes.
Small changes.
Daily changes.
Changes to the tape you play in your head.

Knowing is not enough.
You must decide you are worthy.
Worthy of goodness.
Worthy of forgiveness.
Worthy of being loved.

Knowing is not enough.
But you already know that.

January 18

Silence is holy. It draws people together because only those who are comfortable with each other can sit without speaking. This is the great paradox.
—Nicholas Sparks

I could tell you a story of the brokenness I have known.

But my scars say it more beautifully than could my words.

I could tell you a story of the broken roads I have traveled.

But my worn soul says it more honestly than could my words.

I could tell you a story of the loneliness I have felt.

But the tears say it more clearly than could my words.

I could tell you a story of the fears I have been haunted by.

But my trembling heart says it louder than could my words.

I could tell you a story of the ache I have been consumed by.

But my immobility says it more truthfully than could my words.

I could tell you a story of the darkness I have seen.

But my shadows say more hauntingly than could my words.

I could tell you a story of the nightmares I have awaken to.

But my muted screams say it more terrifyingly than could my words.

I could tell you a story of the love I have lost.

But my quiet surrender says it more accurately than could my words.

I could tell you a story. But if you dare to simply hold me in silence, words will not be necessary.

If I were to offer my truth to you,
Which speaks of your worth,
To whisper, "I believe in you,"
To tell of your strength,
Would you hear it?

If I were to offer my love to you,
As a part of the healing,
To fill your heart,
Never wavering,
Would you simply embrace it?

If I, would you?

January 21

*It's probably my job to tell you life isn't fair, but I figure you already know that.
So instead, I'll tell you that hope is precious, and you're right not to give up.*
—C. J. Redwine

You may fear the dream.
You do not give up on your dream.

You may question the path.
You do not give up on your journey.

You may come to the edge.
You do not give up on your ability to soar.

You may struggle to accept the gift.
You do not give up on your blessings.

You may not control the timing.
You do not give up on your now.

You may regret the past.
You do not give up on your future.

You may feel the pain.
You do not give up on your healing.

You may tremble at the unknown.
You do not give up on your truth.

You may never have felt the truest love.
You do not give up on your heart.

You do not give up on you.

January 22

*It is only when we are ready to give up on some things
in our lives that we could receive new things.*
—*Sunday Adelaja*

Dear You,

When you decide your future holds more than your past, so that tomorrow bears all good things;

When you recognize your brokenness was not an ending, but that it is an awakening;

When you see your darkness never enveloped the light, but that hope always shines;

When you can open your self to the possibilities, so that the unknown is not to be feared;

When you accept your own forgiveness, so that grace toward yourself heals;

When you trust your strength to see you through, so that you can stand again;

When you realize your heart never stopped beating, but that it always has room for love;

When you understand you are truly worthy of an unwavering love, and that you always have been;

Then, come home to me. I will be waiting.

Love,

Your life

January 23

My body is precious and not separate from my soul.
—S.A.R.K.

Everybody. Every body. Nobody.

Everybody has their own unique gift.

Every body is a gift to be treasured.

Nobody has the right to steal that.

Everybody has their individual pace.

Every body moves at its own pace.

Nobody has the right to discount that.

Everybody has their own brand of greatness.

Every body is capable of greatness.

Nobody has the right to prevent that.

Everybody is deserving of respect.

Every body is to be respected.

Nobody has the right to alter that.

Everybody is beautiful in their own way.

Every body is simply beautiful.

Nobody has the right to speak against that.

Everybody is somebody worth loving.

Every body is worth loving.

Nobody has the right to deny that.

January 24

Instead of asking what do I want from life, a more powerful
question is what does life want from me?
—Eckhart Tolle

And so I asked...

"Life, what do you want from me?"

And came the reply...

"I want you to believe. In your light, your gifts, your beauty, your self. I want you to believe.

"I want you to give. Give of yourself, give thanks, give hope to others, give your best. I want you to give.

"I want you to make a difference. In the life of a child, in your corner of the world, wherever you go, to whomever you meet. I want you to make a difference.

"I want you to stop. Making excuses for your behavior, doubting the truth, worrying about the uncontrollable, fearing what others might think. I want you to stop.

"I want you to be accepting. Of help, of genuine compliments, of forgiveness, of love. I want you to be accepting.

"I want you to trust. Your strength, your heart, the process, the path. I want you to trust.

"I want you to endlessly pursue. Dreams, unicorns, goose bumps, horizons. I want you to endlessly pursue.

"I want you to be. Humble, kind, grateful, loving. I want you to be."

"I want you to love. Your perfect imperfections, your amazing, beautiful, holy self, unconditionally, unwaveringly. I want you to love.

"I want you to live. With arms and heart wide open, facing forward, as if today were all you have, a life that honors you. I want you to live."

Today, may you set out to do what your life wants from you.

January 25

I have questions. This is another life chat.

Me: I'm glad we have this time to talk; so many questions I have for you.
Life: Tell me, what's been on your mind?

Me: What lesson am I to take from my latest failure?
Life: If there was a lesson, was it really a failure?

Me: What step am I to take now that this path has come to an end?
Life: Did the path end, or do you just need to take another step?

Me: How do I move forward from here?
Life: Do you want to move forward, or are you meant to be here?

Me: When will I realize where it is I am meant to be?
Life: When will you finally realize you already know where you want to be?

Me: How long should I hold on to this dream I have been keeping?
Life: Is the dreaming worth holding on to?

Me: How do I remain unwavering in belief and hope-filled?
Life: Can you ever really afford not to?

Me: Did you really provide any answers?
Life: My child, the simple truth is: only you will be able to find your answers.

January 26

I know now that we never get over great losses; we absorb them
and they carve us into different, often kinder creatures.
—Gail Caldwell

I am being broken. Piece by piece. A little at a time.
Some parts no longer needed.
Guilt, shame, regret, anger.
Yet, the best pieces remain.
Forgiveness, worthiness, understanding, love.
Broken into a better version of me.

I am being carved. Slowly. Painfully.
Excesses slowly etched away.
Jagged edges made smooth.
Time sculpting a different dream.
Shaping a beautiful tomorrow.
Carved into a better version of me.

I am being made to try anew. Awkward. Uncomfortable.
The old ways did not work.
Comfortable equaled settling.
This is now an awkward dance.
Each step taken moves me closer.
To a new and better version of me.

I am being changed. At times unwillingly. At times unknowingly.
The changes are difficult.
Often I feel unwelcome, unwanted.
This is growth; this is learning.
Change must happen, or nothing changes.
Changed into a better version of me.

I am being broken.
I am being carved.
I am being made to try anew.
I am being changed.

Through all of this, I am becoming a better version of me.

January 27

Prayer is not an old woman's idle amusement. Properly understood and applied, it is the most potent instrument of action.
—Mahatma Gandhi

Tonight. My prayers. For you.

I shall not pray you close your eyes to what is.
I shall pray you open them to all that can be.

I shall not pray you simply seek to be comfortable.
I shall pray you have courage to reach for that beyond your comfort zone.

I shall not pray you are never reminded of the pain.
I shall pray you recall the joy you once knew.

I shall not pray your brokenness be undone.
I shall pray you see your beautiful reflection in all the pieces.

I shall not pray you are not alone.
I shall pray you know there is one who would never abandon you.

I shall not pray for freedom from the struggle.
I shall pray the struggle does not become you.

I shall not pray you have an ordinary love.
I shall pray you have an always, in everything, unwavering love.

You are in my prayers.

January 28

And I learned what is obvious to a child. That life is simply a collection
of little lives, each lived one day at a time. That each day should be
spent finding beauty in flowers and poetry and talking to animals.
—*Nicholas Sparks*

You simply have today.

Simply accept, simply aspire.

Simply be, simply breathe.

Simply do, simply dream.

Simply forgive, simply free yourself.

Simply give, simply grow.

Simply love, simply live.

Simply move, simply make peace.

Simply play, simply pray.

Simply smile, simply shine.

Simply try, simply trust.

Simply unwind, simply unfurl.

Simply wander, simply wonder.

You have today. Simply.

January 29

Some lessons can't be taught. They must simply be learned.
—Jodi Picoult

Everything I need to know, I already learned.

* Be kind.

* If given something of value, value it.

* If you break something, fix it.

* It's never too late to say, "I'm sorry."

* It's never too late to start over again.

* The path of least resistance rarely leads you where you need to go.

* Doing something out of convenience is usually the worst reason.

* The difficult things are usually worth the struggle.

* You don't always need to know the answers.

* Faith is a net, so jump.

* Nothing in the past can be undone, but you always have a choice about what you do next.

* Memories sustain us; thus, living is about making something memorable.

* We remember moments of breathlessness, goose bumps, throat lumps, and joyful tears...make those.

* If you miss someone, want someone, love someone, you should tell them.

* Time doesn't heal; you simply find a way to be okay.

* If someone always wants the best for you, they may be the best for you.

* You are always worthy of love.

* You were given the gift of life; how you spend it is a gift you give yourself.

* Some things must remain eternal: hope and love being most important.

January 30

What we do today, echoes forever.
—Eyden I.

I stood at the edge of my cliff and threw my echo into the valley below: "Have I made a difference for another?"

No echo returned. Only silence.

I stood at the edge of my cliff and threw my echo into the valley below: "Have I left another in a better place for having walked with them?"

No echo returned. Only silence.

I stood at the edge of my cliff and threw my echo into the valley below: "Have I loved another unconditionally, unwaveringly, with all of my heart?"

No echo returned. Only silence.

I stood at the edge of my cliff and threw my echo into the valley below: "Will my presence be missed by another?"

No echo returned. Only silence.

I stood at the edge of my cliff and threw my echo into the valley below: "Have I given another the best of me?"

No echo returned. Only silence.

I finally turned and walked away. In silence.

This is the moral of the story: It is not for me to ask my life of such questions. It is for me to live in such a way as to always know the answers.

January 31

Half of what I say is meaningless; but I say it so that the other half may reach you.
—Kahlil Gibran

What I said. And what I meant.

I said, "I am grateful." For your light, your presence in my life, your gifts, your love... for you.

What I meant was, "I love you."

I said, "I miss you." Your smile, voice, fragrance, spirit...your love.

What I meant was, "I love you."

I said, "I am sorry." For words spoken, words never spoken, things done, things never done...for being wrong.

What I meant was, "I love you."

I said, "I understand." What you are going through, what you need, what frightens you, what hurt you...what you cannot say.

What I meant was, "I love you."

I said, "I will be there for you." When you need, when you want, when pain comes, when joy arrives....whenever.

What I meant was, "I love you."

I said, "I love you." As you are, scars and beauty marks, unwaveringly, unconditionally...all of you.

What I meant was, "For always."

February 1

Your mission: Be so busy loving your life that you
have no time for hate, regret or fear.
—Karen Salmansohn

Dear Life,

I love you.

You took me to the brink. Of ecstasy. Of brokenness. Of reason.

You made me doubt myself. My gifts. My resolve. My heart.

You tore me open. Exposed my weakness. Dipped me in pain. Brought me to my knees.

You are unanswered questions. Am I enough? Is this worth it? Why?

You are like nothing I know. Beauty. Simplicity. Holy.

You changed my course. My steps. My heartbeat. My very life.

You cannot be seen with the eyes. You must be experienced. Tasted. Lived.

You feel like home to me. Comforting. Familiar. Inviting.

I'm coming back home to you. Once more.

I love you. Still.

Love,

Me

February 2

There had been times when he knew, somewhere in him, that he would get used to it, whatever it was, because he had learnt that some hard things became softer after a very little while.
—Nick Hornby

There are times it is not about the difficult moments, but the moments you overcame the difficult.

There are times it is not about the place you take, but the place it took you.

There are times it is not about the hills you were forced to climb, but who the hills forced you to become.

There are times it is not about the medal, but about how your mettle was tested.

There are times it is not about who bested you, but about if you gave your best.

There are times it is not about effort invested, but about knowing you are worth the investment.

There are times it is not about running for yourself, but about not running from yourself.

There are times it is not about going it alone when the pain arrives, but about who will come along with you.

There are times it is not about the time you finished, but about the time you had finishing.

February 3

Loving yourself means being your own best friend, standing by yourself at all times, including times of failure; being there for yourself no matter what.
—Anita Moorjani

Dear You,

I've been watching you.
I've watched as you've struggled.
I've watched as you've succeeded.
I've watched as you've grown.
I've watched as you've become stronger.

I've been praying for you.
I've prayed for your safety.
I've prayed for your health.
I've prayed for you joy.
I've prayed for you peace.

I've been believing in you.
I've believed in your light.
I've believed in your courage.
I've believed in your capacity to overcome.
I've believed in your dreams.

I've been celebrating you.
I've celebrated your steps forward.
I've celebrated your effort.
I've celebrated your journey.
I've celebrated your triumphs.

I've been loving you.
I've loved you at your worst.
I've loved you at your best.
I've loved you unconditionally.
I've loved you unwaveringly.

I've been there for you.
I've been there during the darkness.
I've been there when no one else was.
I've been there in the silence.
I've been there whenever you needed.

Love, Your self

February 4

When you get stranded, the way to start moving again
is not to search for an answer, but to find
a new question to which your life can be the answer.
—Jennifer Krause

Of all the questions I must ask myself, this must be the most essential: what questions shall my life be the answer to?

What choice did I make, helplessness or hopefulness?

Do difficulties define me or do they refine me?

Am I a victim or a hero in my life's story?

Have I abandoned or remained faithful to my dreams?

Was a single life made better for my having lived?

When darkness arrives, as it shall, did I shine a light?

Did I use the gifts granted me?

Do I simply still believe?

Are forgiveness, compassion, kindness, and unwavering love evidence that I was here?

If these are to be my questions, I know how I must live my life. Lest I be stranded.

February 5

You may encounter many defeats, but you must not be defeated. In fact, it may be necessary to encounter the defeats, so you can know who you are, what you can rise from, how you can still come out of it.
—Maya Angelou

I came up short.
Somehow, I failed.
The dream slowly slipped away.

I was not good enough.
An unspoken truth.
In the silence, it screams at me.

I was passed by.
Another claimed the prize.
My best was deemed unworthy.

I know what must be done.
Find no fault, place no blame.
Learn, grow, improve.

I dare to start over.
Begin from the beginning.
Patient, forgiving, unwavering.

I will rebuild from scratch.
Starting from the inside.
Strength, trust, hope.

I believe in the improbable.
Do not fear the impossible.
Faith, the key I hold.

I cannot alter yesterday.
Yet I can determine my tomorrow.
I will find my way home again.

I know what I seek.
If it is meant to be.
This dream will not expire.

I will be ready.
When the moment arrives again.
And this time, I will not fail.

February 6

Charm is simply a matter of being yourself. Your uniqueness is your power.
—Keith Ferrazzi

Hey you,

Yes, you. I'm talking to you. Writing to you. Looking right at you. I hope I have your attention. I wanted to say a few things.

You are...

...amazing

...beautiful

...blessed

...worthy

...capable

...unique

...special

...strong

...brilliant

...gifted

...awesome

...enough

...loved

...holy

Just thought I would remind you.

Now, go about the business of simply being you.

February 7

Now I know what a ghost is. Unfinished business, that's what.
—Salman Rushdie

I awake.
To the darkness.
The world still sleeps.
But I am restless.

I awake.
To the quiet.
The road is silent.
But I hear it calling.

I awake.
To the tiredness.
The body is weary.
But I must rise.

I awake.
To the aches.
The muscles ever bruised.
But I cannot remain still.

I awake.
To the numbness.
The legs struggle to feel.
But I have miles to conquer.

I awake.
To the excuses.
The opt-out is ever present.
But I choose results.

I awake.
To the knowing.
The training takes a toll.
But I refuse to fail.

I awake.
To silence the ghost.

February 8

If you feel lost, disappointed, hesitant, or weak, return to yourself, to who you are, here and now and when you get there, you will discover yourself, like a lotus flower in full bloom, even in a muddy pond, beautiful and strong.
—*Masaru Emoto*

This. This is a letter to the me I once knew.

Dear Me,

I miss you. How your voice whispered a pride in me. How you spoke of your love for me. I miss how you once talked to me. For the words you speak of me are all that matter.

I miss you. How you saw beyond the scars. How you could see the beauty in me. I miss how I once appeared in your eyes. For the way you see me, is all that matters.

I miss you. How you celebrated me. How you knew of my gifts. I miss how you once understood the wonder and awe of me. For the way you feel about me is all that matters.

I miss you. How you thought I could achieve the impossible. How you trusted the wings I have been given. I miss how you once believed in me. For your belief in me is all that matters.

I miss you. How you so valued me. How unwavering your love was. I miss how you once loved me. For your love for me is all that matters.

I miss you. It is time to return home to me.

Love,

Your self

February 9

Attitude is a choice. Happiness is a choice. Optimism is a choice.
Kindness is a choice. Giving is a choice. Respect is a choice.
Whatever choice you make makes you. Choose wisely.
—Roy T. Bennett

Head down.
I focus on the very next step.
For there awaits everything I seek.
I pay attention to the details.
For there are found the answers.
I move forward.
For there all finish lines are attained.

Quietly.
I believe in my strength.
For it has never failed me.
I go about the work of growing.
For it is my actions, not my words.
I speak my truths.
For even in whispers, I hear all I say.

Determined.
I am accepting of the difficult.
For I did not come here for easy.
I am accepting of the path.
For I trust it to lead me home.
I am accepting of the wall.
For I know it can be moved.

Unwavering.
I face the unknowns.
For I am greater than my fears.
I pursue my dreams.
For I am worthy of them.
I choose to love.
For I am simply following my heart.

Head down. Quiet. Determined. Unwavering.

These.
The choices I have made.
About how I shall live this life.

February 10

If you live the questions, life will move you into the answers.
—Deepak Chopra

At the end of each day, life has questions. I have answers. This is another life chat.

Life: What footprint did you leave?
Me: None. I walked gently this day.

Life: What path did you choose?
Me: The one that challenged me.

Life: When challenged, how did you respond?
Me: With a quiet dignity and belief.

Life: What did you offer another?
Me: Time and understanding.

Life: What did you offer yourself?
Me: Grace and forgiveness.

Life: What did you hold on to?
Me: The hope I have. The dream I seek.

Life: What did you let go of?
Me: The fear I have. The burden I carry.

Life: What did you give?
Me: The very best I had.

Life: What did you learn today?
Me: As I change me, my world changes.

Life: What defined you today?
Me: That my love for you did not waver.

Life: It has been a good day.
Me. Yes, it has been.

February 11

Dear Life,

I want to be heard. My cries. My truth. My song. No longer silent.

I want to hear: "I'm sorry." "I choose you." "I love you." "I always will."

I want to be seen. As beautiful. As worthy. As special. No longer invisible.

I want to see. Beyond your darkness. Your tomorrows. The dream I hold. The best of you.

I want to be fought for. Stood up for. Lifted when I am weak. Understood when I am broken. For I am worth it.

I want to fight. The urge to run away. The giving up. The comfortable. The settling.

I want to be embraced. Hugged when I am hurting. Held when I am afraid. Wrapped up even as I push you away. Pulled close as I dream.

I want to embrace. Each and every moment. The challenges before me. This broken road. The journey that waits.

I want to be made to feel. Valued. As a priority. Wanted. As though I matter.

I want to feel. Breathless. A trembling. Goose bumps. Holy.

I want to be loved. At my worst. At my best. As I am. Unconditionally.

I want to love. Without fear. With all my heart. Unwavering. And to have my love received.

You may think I want too much. Yet, all that I now want, Is all that I have given.

Love,

Me

February 12

We've all got both light and dark inside us. What matters is the
part we choose to act on. That's who we really are.
—J. K. Rowling

When I was four, they denied my family housing because of the color of my skin.

I could have learned how to hate. Instead, I decided if you ever noticed my color, it would be because of my beautiful light.

When I was eleven, they teased me so unmercifully for being short, I left school in tears.

I could have learned intolerance. Instead, I decided if you ever measured my stature, it would be by the size of my heart and depth of my character.

When I was eighteen, they turned off the heat in our house because we could not afford to pay the bills.

I could have learned to ask for a handout. Instead, I decided if you ever saw my hand extended, it would be to help another up.

When I was twenty-three, they told me I had no future and would never amount to much.

I could have learned to accept failure. Instead, I decided if you ever spoke of my failings, it would be because I dared to do the impossible.

When I was thirty-nine, they believed I would end up completely alone.

I could have learned to settle. Instead, I decided if you ever wondered why I walk alone, it would be in search of someone grateful for the gifts and love I offer.

When I was fifty, they belittled my dreams as being unrealistic, for I was too old.

I could have learned to compromise. Instead, I decided If ever you doubted your dreams, it would be me who would cheer you on toward yours.

I could have learned so much. Instead, I decided if you ever looked back on my life, it would be to see how I decided to become the me I am today.

February 13

And that's when I knew that I was going to be okay.
—Sherman Alexie

Pain.
Known its company
Taught me I was alive
And thus, I will be okay.

Tears.
Tasted their bitterness
Learned to value the sweet
And thus, I will be okay.

Darkness.
Seen gloom in my soul
Made me look for the light
And thus, I will be okay.

Solitude.
Walked a lonely path
Helped me find comfort in my skin
And thus, I will be okay.

Regret.
Carried this burden
Gave me strength to forgive
And thus, I will be okay.

Love.
Let it slip through my hands
Left a fingerprint on my heart
And thus, I will be okay.

Whatever it is, you will be okay, my friend.

February 14

The only thing that holds you back from getting what you
want is paying attention to what you don't want.
—Abraham-Hicks

Consider all those things that hold you back.

Mistakes.

Those things you should finally forgive yourself for.

Those things that do not mean failure.

Burdens.

Things which cannot be altered.

Things you can simply let go of.

Obstacles.

The things you alone put in front of you.

The things you can easily go around.

Fears.

Of things which often never occur.

Of things only imagined.

Perhaps it is time to reconsider those things and come to finally realize: there is really nothing to hold you back.

February 15

The most effective attitude to adopt is one of supreme acceptance.
—Robert Greene

When I accept where I am,

I need no longer regret where I once stood.

When I accept how I arrived at this place,

I need no longer fear how I will move on from here.

When I accept that I need to make changes in my life,

I need no longer cling to what does not serve my good.

When I accept what I am capable of,

I need no longer make excuses for what I am unable yet to do.

When I accept that I have fought to be me,

I need no longer feel shame for the scars I bear.

When I accept who I am,

I need no longer apologize for simply being me.

February 16

My scars remind me that I did indeed survive my deepest wounds. That in itself is an accomplishment. And they bring to mind something else, too. They remind me that the damage life has inflicted on me has, in many places, left me stronger and more resilient. What hurt me in the past has actually made me better equipped to face the present.
—Steve Goodier

My scars. They tell a story.

Of how I did not run from my fears. Of how I chose to do more than survive.

Of how I decided I was worth the fight.

My scars. They tell a story.

Of when I dared face my demons. Of when I walked straight into the fire.

Of when I announced, "I will not be broken."

My scars. They tell a story.

Of where I once stood. Of where I could not remain.

Of where I learned to become a warrior.

My scars. They tell a story.

Of what I refused to let defeat me. Of what I cannot always speak.

Of what I overcame.

My scars. They tell a story.

Of who I was. Of who I am.

Of who I fought to become.

My scars. They tell a story.

If you listen, you will hear of a life truly lived.

February 17

Like a butterfly burrowing from its chrysalis, so shall you find
your wings, if you only take the time to find yourself.
—L. J. Vanier

I am headed to somewhere I've never been before.

Just beyond the doubt.

And there, I will find my truth.

I am headed to somewhere I've never been before.

Just beyond the fear.

And there, I will find my courage.

I am headed to somewhere I've never been before.

Just beyond the shadows.

And there, I will find my light.

I am headed to somewhere I've never been before.

Just beyond the breaking.

And there, I will find my strength.

I am headed to somewhere I've never been before.

Just beyond the wall.

And there, I will find my possibilities.

I am headed to somewhere I've never been before.

And there, I will find me.

February 18

No amount of security is worth the suffering of a mediocre life
chained to a routine that has killed your dreams.
—Maya Mendoza

Stay free, stay wild
Be willing, be open
Let loose your inner child
Allow the happiness to win

Open your heart's cage
Fear not the breaking
Time to turn the page
Love soothes the aching

Live not a life in chains
Your spirit longs to be free
Temporary are the pains
Forever is the victory

Do not let them tame you
Always struggle to be free
To yourself be always true
Never let them hold the key

February 19

We are our choices.
—Jean-Paul Sartre

This is your pep talk.

You have a choice.
Fall forward, or fall behind.
Get moving, or get left behind.

You have a choice.
Fail trying, or fail to try.
Try again, or try living with "what if."

You have a choice.
Step forward, or step aside.
Step it up, or step down.

You have a choice.
Find your reason, or find your excuse.
Give your best, or give your excuse.

You have a choice.
Be hopeful, or be doubtful.
Believe you will, or doubt you can.

You have a choice.
Be open to change or remain the same.
Update your status, or settle for the status quo.

You have a choice.

Work to overcome, or be overcome by the work.

Overwhelm the day, or be overwhelmed by the day.

You have a choice. What's it going to be?

You've just been pep-talked.

February 20

Among my stillness was a pounding heart.
—Shannon A. Thompson

I said, "I am so very lost."
"Follow me," came the reply.

I said, "I am so very broken."
"Let me heal you," came the reply.

I said, "I cannot go on."
"I will not let you fail," came the reply.

I said, "I am so very weak."
"I am your strength," came the reply.

I said, "I feel only emptiness."
"Place your hand on me," came the reply.

I said nothing at all.
And the beating of my heart broke the silence.

February 21

Sometimes, the words we keep in our hearts, no matter
how unmistakable, are best left unspoken.
—Jourdane Erasquin

If your words are not of peace,

They are too often used as weapons.

If your words are not of hope,

They are incapable of offering light.

If your words are not of forgiveness,

They are used only to place blame.

If your words are not of truth,

They are not an essential part of the story.

If your words are not of love,

They are not ever able to conquer hate.

February 22

Being grateful does not mean that everything is necessarily good. It just means that you can accept it as a gift.
—Roy T. Bennett

Broken and bent
Down on my knees
Softly kissed the earth
Grateful to have traveled this far

Broken and bent
Down on my knees
Softly asked forgiveness
Grateful to have another chance

Broken and bent
Down on my knees
Softly heard my beating heart
Grateful to have known of love

Broken and bent
Down on my knees
Softly whispered a prayer
Grateful to have been given this day

Broken and bent
Arose from my knees
Softly nodded my head
Knowing that gratitude saved me

February 23

The frankest and freest and most private product of
the human mind and heart is a love letter.
— Mark Twain

Many days, life writes its love letter to me.

This day, I wrote a love letter to my life.

Dear Life,

I know there is little you can offer to me.

For with each passing breath, you are becoming more beautifully fragile.

For with each passing breath, you are slowly slipping away from me.

Thus, with the breaths I have remaining, these I shall offer unto you.

Patience to allow you to gently unfurl.

Faith that shows I shall trust your path.

Quiet so that your intentions may be heard.

Gratitude for the beauty you have shown.

Gentleness as a way to walk with you.

Forgiveness so that I may not regret.

Humility before the wonder of you.

Hope for just one more day with you.

For as I lie in the darkness and silence this night, with each passing breath, you will know it was always an unwavering love I offered unto you.

And it is all you have ever asked of me.

Love,

Me

February 24

Yes: I am a dreamer. For a dreamer is one who can only find his way by moonlight,
and his punishment is that he sees the dawn before the rest of the world.
—Oscar Wilde

Dear You,

I've been waiting for you.
To join the chase.

I've been hoping for you.
To believe in me.

I've been sending you messages.
Saying this is possible.

I've been anticipating.
The day you arrive.

I've been praying for you.
To stop being afraid.

I've been imagining you.
Fully embracing me.

I've been whispering your name.
Wanting your heart to hear me.

I've been dreaming of you.
Falling completely in love with me.

I've been waiting for you.
To finally wake up.

Love,

Your dream

February 25

I'd like to take a long walk, to the edge of something.
—Arthur K. Flam

So many times, I have walked to the edge.
Of my comfort. To face the changes.

So many times, I have walked to the edge.
Of my knowing. To face the unknown.

So many times, I have walked to the edge.
Of my courage. To face the fear.

So many times, I have walked to the edge.
Of my strength. To face the weakness.

So many times, I have walked to the edge.
Of my light. To face the darkness.

So many times, I have walked to the edge.
Of my used-to-be. To face what will be.

So many times, I have walked to the edge.
Of my being. To face who I am to become.

And each time, it is from there that I have launched myself.

February 26

You will survive anything if you live your life from the point of view of truth.
—Oprah Winfrey

Life has a different point of view.
This is another life chat.

Me: My hope has been diminished.
Life: What is immeasurable can never be reduced.

Me: My wounds have been ripped open.
Life: What has been healed will not bleed.

Me: My faith has been shaken.
Life: What foundation is built on bedrock shall never tremble.

Me: My tomorrow has been altered.
Life: What has not arrived is not able to be changed.

Me: My gifts have been refused.
Life: What is given with love is always received.

Me: My fire has been extinguished.
Life: What is fed can never die.

Me: My trust has been stolen.
Life: What is given freely cannot be stolen.

Me: My heart has been broken.

Life: What continues to work is not broken.

Me: We just don't see things from the same point of view.

Life: True. For you are focused on looking *in*, while I am looking *out* for you.

February 27

Our deepest wounds surround our greatest gifts.
—Ken Page

The open wound is not a sign of weakness.
For you stood before the source of your pain.
And you did not bow before it.
There is strength in receiving this wound.

The open wound is not a sign of brokenness.
For you faced the demons that cut you.
And you did not surrender.
There is courage in receiving this wound.

The open wound is not a sign of emptiness.
For you opened yourself to the possibilities.
And you did not fear.
There is growth in receiving this wound.

The open wound is not a sign of failure.
For you accepted the challenge laid before you.
And you did not waver.
There is hope in receiving this wound.

The open wound, it is a sign.
Strength. Courage. Growth. Hope.

February 28

Dear Life,

You tried to steal some things from me.
Things valuable, rare, hard to replace.
Harder to live without. Trust, love, hope.

You humbled me. But I am one of a kind.
For I will learn to trust again. I will not let love waver.
I will remain hope-filled.

You tried to cheat me out of some things.
Things I sought for so long.
How I did search. Belief, dreams, home.

You humbled me. But I am one of a kind.
For I will still believe. I will dream again.
I will find my way back home.

You tried to lie to me about some things.
Things I held as truths.
Pieces of me. My worth, light, beauty.

You humbled me. But I am one of a kind.
For I will not be diminished. I will shine again.
I will be seen as beautiful.

You humbled me.
But I...am one of a kind.

Always,

Me

March 1

Life's under no obligation to give us what we expect.
—Margaret Mitchell

It was not courage that brought you here.
It's what you did when you were afraid.

It was not faith that brought you here.
It's what you did when you did not believe.

It was not easy that brought you here.
It's what you did when the struggle set in.

It was not victory that brought you here.
It's what you did when the surrender arrived.

It was not answers that brought you here.
It's what you did when you did not know.

It was not having it all together that brought you here.
It's what you did when you were broken.

It was not life's smile that brought you here.
It's what you did when life kicked you in the teeth.

In the end, life—it's what you did.

March 2

When their hearts close, love more; when they forget the thank
yous, do not stop giving; when they are taken by darkness, be the
warrior of light. In your strength, lies hope for the world.
—*Brendon Burchard*

Now, more than ever.

A closed heart cannot be forced open.
A closed heart cannot be broken open.
A closed heart can only be loved open.
Love more.

A gift given unselfishly asks no thank-you.
A gift given freely asks no thank-you.
A gift can only be given unconditionally
Give more.

Darkness cannot be contained.
Darkness cannot be isolated.
Darkness can only disappear with light.
Shine more.

Now, more than ever.
Your strength is needed.
For in you lies the hope for all.

Love. Give. Shine. More.

March 3

*It shouldn't be easy to be amazing. Then everything would be. It's the
things you fight for and struggle with before earning that have the
greatest worth. When something's difficult to come by, you'll do that
much more to make sure it's even harder—or impossible—to lose.*
—Sarah Dessen

There is something you should know.

Your strength leaves me in awe.
Your vulnerability draws me in.

Your light leaves me in wonder.
Your shadows captivate me.

Your voice leaves me without words.
Your silence resonates with me.

Your courage leaves me steadied.
Your fears tell me I do not walk alone.

Your beauty leaves me humbled.
Your scars tell me you are a warrior.

Your resolve leaves me to question mine.
Your failures free me to be imperfect.

Your story leaves me hope-filled.
Your unwritten chapters inspire me.

There is something you should know.

It is all of you that is worthy of love.
Even the parts you do not always love.

March 4

Greatness is not found in possessions, power, position, or prestige.
It is discovered in goodness, humility, service, and character.
—William Arthur Ward

Greatness is not found. It is discovered.

Be good.
Be humble.
Offer service.
Offer hope.
Demonstrate character.
Demonstrate patience.
Say a prayer.
Say, "I love you."

Give of your time.
Give of yourself.
Practice peace.
Practice faith.
Speak softly.
Speak gently.
Raise your bar.
Raise up another.

Shine your light.
Shine your love.
Take the high road.
Take nothing for granted.
Be a friend.

Be the change.
Give without taking.
Give without conditions.

Listen with intent.
Listen without judgment.
Show you care.
Show your smile.
Love your neighbor.
Love yourself.

Greatness is not found. It is discovered.
Go discover your greatness.

March 5

My letter of forgiveness. My letter of thanks.

Dear Life,

I am thankful for the brokenness.
For times I have known only emptiness.
For losing that I held so close.
For my heart must have known love.

I am thankful for dreams lost.
For the broken paths I have traveled.
Without a map to chart my way.
For my heart must have known love.

I am thankful for the falls taken.
When I believed I could not rise again.
Yet each time, I was able to find my feet.
For my heart must have known love.

I am thankful for scars I have been given.
Whether self-inflicted or brought by another.
I fought for something of value.
For my heart must have known love.

I am thankful for the tears I have cried.
Whether out of joy or sorrow.
There was laughter and pain.
For my heart must have known love.

I am thankful. For everything.
For my heart has known love.

Love,

Me

March 6

Dreams come true; without that possibility, nature would not incite us to have them.
—John Updike

This dream I hold.

I did not wish for it.
I worked for it.

I did not fear it.
I refused to bow before it.

I did not quit on it.
I gave my everything to it.

I did not stop pursuing it.
I wandered endlessly in search of it.

I did not turn away from it.
I watched over it.

I did not cheat on it.
I always honored it.

I did not abandon it.
I, even in the darkness, held it.

I did not lose faith in it.
I still believe in it.

I did not simply want it.
I unconditionally loved it.

This dream, I hold.

March 7

Sometimes, simply by sitting, the soul collects wisdom.
—Zen proverb

There are times I sit in the darkness.

To listen to my ghosts encroach upon me.
To listen to my life say, "You are a light."

There are times I sit in the emptiness.

To listen to my fears fill the spaces.
To listen to my life say, "Be not afraid."

There are times I sit in the pain.

To listen to my tears trace these scars.
To listen to my life say, "You are a warrior."

There are times I sit in the stillness.

To listen to my thoughts speak their lies.
To listen to my life say, "Quiet the noise."

There are times I sit in the wonder.

To listen to my questions without answers.
To listen to my life say, "You already know."

There are times I sit in the silence.

To listen to my heart drum its broken beat.
To listen to my life say, "It will be okay."

There are times I sit.

And my life simply exhales.

March 8

These are life's ingredients.
This is another life chat.

Me: I have wandered for so long.
Life: To find what you are meant to become requires time.

Me: I have been consumed by flames.
Life: To forge you into what you are meant to become requires trial by fire.

Me: I have known many difficulties.
Life: To grow into what you are meant to become requires dealing with pressure.

Me: I have not found what I am looking for.
Life: To discover what you are meant to become requires patience.

Me: I have never known my own worth.
Life: To understand what you are meant to become requires knowing you are valuable.

Me: Can you not simply tell me what I am meant to become?
Life: I have given you all the ingredients.

Me: Time. Fire. Pressure. Patience. Value. What are these to make of me?
Life: Dear sweet child, don't you see? Through all of this, you are becoming a diamond.

March 9

I don't deserve your love, but you give it to me anyway.
—Paul Van Dyk

You deserve to be loved, simply as you are.
Not just when you are at your best.

You deserve to be loved, even when you feel broken.
Not just when you are whole.

You deserve to be loved, even when your steps falter.
Not just when your path is easy.

You deserve to be loved, even when you are lost.
Not just when your searching is over.

You deserve to be loved, even when in the depths of your despair.
Not just when you know joy.

You deserve to be loved, even when you mess up.
Not just when you are trying to be perfect.

You deserve to be loved, even when you have nothing to offer in return.
Not just when you have something to give.

You deserve to be loved, always.
Not just when it is convenient for another.

You deserve to be loved, even when you do not feel as if you are worthy of love.
You deserve to be loved.

March 10

Do the thing and you will have the power.
—Ralph Waldo Emerson

I woke up today and simply asked myself, "What can I do for another?"

I can sit silently, so another may simply tell of their story.

I can offer my hand, so another may simply know what kindness feels like.

I can shine a light, so another may simply have something to move toward.

I can make sure to smile, so another may simply find their own.

I can be strong enough for two, so another may simply have someone to lean on.

I can enter gently into their day, so another can be comforted by my presence.

I can give unconditionally, so another may simply understand what true love looks like.

I woke up today and simply asked myself, "What can I do for another?"

There is so much I can do.

Let me get on with doing it.

March 11

Speaking kind words starts a wave of love in motion
that brings more love upon your shores.
—Molly Friedenfeld

Love has a language all its own.

If love were spoken in but two letters, it would be "us."
For love speaks of us, shines a light on us, and keeps us always.

If love were spoken in but three letters, it would be "you."
For love puts you first, makes you a priority, honors you.

If love were spoken in but four letters, it would be "time."
For love makes time, gives of its time, exceeds even time.

If love were spoken in but five letters, it would be "trust."
For love grows in trust, requires trust, and is set free with trust.

If love were spoken in but six letters, it would be "smiles."
For love is the cause of the most beautiful smiles, creates unexpected smiles, and delivers the most genuine smiles.

If love were spoken in but seven letters, it would be "forgive."
For love can simply forgive, will forgive without cost, and will always forgive.

If love were spoken in but eight letters, it would be "kindness."
For love is an act of kindness, is guided by kindness, and knows only kindness.

Love. It is spoken in so many simple ways.

March 12

All you have been waiting for is your own permission.
—Pat Rodegast

You are allowed:

To be broken
To feel whole again
To not know
To find your answers
To be angry
To be calm
To feel lost
To find your way
To sit in the despair
To experience joy
To hate where you are
To know love once more
To shut out the world
To welcome one in
To be confused
To have clarity
To not be okay
To simply be okay
To break down
To stand again
To hold on so tight
To slowly let go
To rage
To surrender

To blame yourself
To forgive yourself
To wander lost
To finally come home
To want things how they used to be
To want to start this life anew
To lose hope
To have something to believe in
To say good-bye
To embrace hello
To be a walking contradiction
To be completely you.

You are allowed.
And you need no other's permission, but your own.

March 13

None of us knows what might happen even the next minute, yet we
still go forward. Because we have trust. Because we have faith.
—Paulo Coelho

Trust your light.
It cannot be dimmed.

Trust your courage.
It is in there.

Trust your strength.
It will see you through.

Trust your path.
It will lead you where you are to go.

Trust your unfolding.
It will reveal you.

Trust your heart.
It speaks your answers.

Trust yourself.
It is the greatest act of love.

Trust your love.
It is your truth.

March 14

When it's hard, that's when you know you're making progress.
—P. J. Brust

When the questions are most difficult, that's when you shall find your truest answers.

When the pain is at its greatest, that's when you realize what shall heal you.

When the darkness is deepest, that's when you know the dawn shall soon break.

When the fall seems so scary, that's when you are about to be caught.

When the road is broken and uncertain, that's when you shall be led home.

When the heart is shattered open, that's when light and love can now enter.

When the hardest times arrive, yet you keep moving forward, that's when you are making progress.

March 15

Love is patient.
—1 Corinthians 13:4–8

I will wait. Until all time passes.
Simply to be with you. If only for but a moment.

I will wait. Forever in the shadows.
Simply to bathe in your light. If only for but a moment.

I will wait. Always wandering alone.
Simply to come home to you. If only for but a moment.

I will wait. Constantly invisible.
Simply to be seen in your eyes. If only for but a moment.

I will wait. Because you may need.
Simply to be needed by you. If only for but a moment.

I will wait. As only love can.
Simply to be loved by you. If only for but a moment.

I will wait. Simply. Gently. Always.
For love is patient.

March 16

Every day is a good day. There is something to learn, care [about,] and celebrate.
—Amit Ray

The sun came up.
Again.
It's a good day.

You are breathing.
Deeply.
It's a good day.

You get to choose.
Everything.
It's a good day.

You are moving.
Forward.
It's a good day.

You have what it takes.
Hope.
It's a good day.

You have what you need.
Faith.
It's a good day.

You are beautiful.
Naturally.
It's a good day.

You are not alone.
Ever.
It's a good day.

You are loved.
Always.
It's a good day.

March 17

I took your darkness, led you here.
To a place of beauty.
But I cannot make you see the light.

I took your sorrow, led you here.
To a place of happiness.
But I cannot make you feel the joy.

I took your truth, led you here.
To a place of dreams.
But I cannot make you believe.

I took your hand, led you here.
To a place beyond yesterday.
But I cannot make you leap.

I took your time, led you here.
To a place you longed for.
But I cannot make you stay.

I took your heart, led you here.
To a place called home.
But I cannot make you love.

I gave you all I have, led you here.
To a place with everything.
But the rest is up to you.

March 18

It is an absolute human certainty that no one can know his own beauty
or perceive a sense of his own worth until it has been reflected back
to him in the mirror of another loving, caring human being.
—John Joseph Powell

When you feel as if nobody sees the beautiful you,

When you feel as if nobody cares about you,

When you feel as if nobody is standing beside you,

When you feel as if nobody believes in you,

When you feel as if nobody is thinking of you,

When you feel as if nobody understands you,

When you feel as if nobody wants to be with you,

When you feel as if nobody loves you,

Remember this: Somebody would give everything to be your nobody.

March 19

When you graduate from "Being in Love" to "Loving Someone" you understand—
Love is not about owning, Love is about wanting the best for them, It's about
seeing or Helping them achieve great heights, with or without you.
—Wordions

Someone wants the best for you.
Time. To heal.
Freedom. From pain.
Joy. Overwhelming.

Someone wants the best for you.
Patience. With yourself.
Forgiveness. Of yourself.
Grace. For yourself.

Someone wants the best for you.
Space. To find you.
Closeness. To hold you.
Faith. To guide you.

Someone wants the best for you.
Strength. Each day.
Growth. Each day.
Progress. Each day.

Someone wants the best for you.
Light. From inside.
Love. Unconditional.
Happiness. Complete.

Someone want the best for you.
Dreams. To come true.
Belief. In the dream.
Life. The one you dream of.

Someone wants the best for you,
And when you find that someone,
Don't ever let them go.

March 20

Everything you want lies on the other side of learning to trust yourself. Take a chance. Have faith. You already know who you are, what you want, and where you want to go.
—Vironika Tugaleva

When given the chance to shine a light
Take it
Cast no shadows

When given the chance to remove the doubt
Take it
Become transparent

When given the chance to apologize
Take it
Speak words that heal

When given the chance to make amends
Take it
Act to right the wrong

When given a chance to be trusted once more
Take it
Honor the gift given

When given the chance to forgive
Take it
Genuinely let it go

When given the chance to start anew
Take it
Move forward from this place

When given the chance to love as you have been loved
Take it
Simply give the best you have

You always have a chance.
Take it.

March 21

All the art of living lies in the fine mingling of letting go and holding on.
—Henry Ellis

I have questions. Life has answers. This is another life chat.

Me: How do you let go of the past?
Life: You simply place your faith in today.

Me: How do you let go of the pain?
Life: You simply surrender to the healing.

Me: How do you let go of the burden you've been given?
Life: You simply put it down.

Me: How do you let go of the lies?
Life: You simply stop telling them to yourself.

Me: How do you let go of what you desperately cling to?
Life: You simply unclench your grip.

Me: How do you let go of a broken dream?
Life: You simply open your eyes.

Me: How do you let go of your heart's hope?
Life: You simply don't.

Me: How do you know what to let go of and what to hold on to?
Life: You simply ask, "Does it serve my good?"

March 22

One day someone is going to hug you so tight, that all
of your broken pieces fit back together.
—Anonymous

If I could hug you, it would be until you could stand once more on your own.
So you know you have my support.

If I could hug you, it would be until the tears dried.
So you know I will not turn away when it is difficult.

If I could hug you, it would be until you felt the pieces coming together again.
So you know you are not broken.

If I could hug you, it would be until you could feel my heartbeat.
So you know you are loved.

If I could hug you, I would not let go.
For you should know you are always held in my heart, thoughts, and prayers.

March 23

Now I feel free, and hope is creeping back. Maybe because I'm
paying attention to what I have rather than what's missing.
—Doug Cooper

The breaking dawn to start your day

A cleansing rain to cool the heat

The sound of children laughing

A wagging tail to welcome you home

The taste of cold lemonade

A call from your mom just because

The stars on a cloudless night

A favorite old song on the radio

The breeze through the kitchen window

A random act of kindness from a stranger

The smell of a Sunday barbeque

The silent prayers said for you

A setting sun as your day winds down

The cool of the other side of the pillow

A chance to witness it all again

The world says, "I love you" in so many ways.

I hope you are paying attention.

March 24

I have come to accept the feeling of not knowing where I am going. And I have trained myself to love it. Because it is only when we are suspended in mid-air with no landing in sight, that we force our wings to unravel and alas begin our flight.
—C. JoyBell C.

Amid the silence,
Answers can be heard.

Amid the darkness,
Light can be seen.

Amid the fear,
Courage can be found.

Amid the doubt,
Trust can be gained.

Amid the solitude,
Comfort can be present.

Amid the battle,
Peace can be sought.

Amid the hopelessness,
Hope can be called upon.

Amid the brokenness,
Healing can begin.

Whatever you are in the middle of, you must always trust:
What you need, also exists there.

March 25

Opportunities are like sunrises. If you wait too long, you miss them.
—William Arthur Ward

There are times life asks only questions, yet leads me to my answers.
This is another life chat.

Me: I want my dreams to be realized.
Life: What are you waiting for?

Me: To not be so afraid.
Life: What does it feel like to be afraid?

Me: You tremble.
Life: Could it be you are simply being shaken awake?

Me: You lose your breath.
Life: Could it be a reminder to just exhale?

Me: You feel your heartbeat in your chest.
Life: Could it be a signal that you are fully alive?

Me: That is what fear feels like.
Life: Are you sure that is fear?

Me: I have felt this way every time I arrive at the crossroad in my life.
Life: The trembling, the breathlessness, the pounding heart?

Me: Yes.
Life: Did you ever think it is not fear you are feeling?

Me: What else could it be?
Life: Could it be this is how love feels?

Me: What if you are wrong?
Life: What if *you* are?

Me: Then I have let so much slip away.
Life: So I will ask again, "What are you waiting for?"

March 26

I attribute my success to this:—I never gave or took an excuse.
—Florence Nightingale

I woke up to the chiming of the alarm clock.
I have no excuse for not taking advantage of the time given me this day.

I woke up to the singing of the birds.
I have no excuse for not being a soothing voice in this day.

I woke up to the morning sun.
I have no excuse for not seeing beauty in this day.

I woke up to the endless possibilities.
I have no excuse for not achieving what I want in this day.

I woke up to the clean slate of a new day.
I have no excuse for soiling it with the messes of yesterday.

I woke up in love with my everything.
I have no excuse for not living in the love I have for this day.

I woke up. I have no excuse.

March 27

How far are you willing to go to create the life you want?
—Gina Greenlee

Life's most repeated question: Are you willing?

Are you willing to chase that which is unseen, unknown?

Are you willing to track down your greatest dreams?

Are you willing to run without fear of what others might think?

Are you willing to pull yourself back up?

Are you willing to hold on tight?

Are you willing to trust your strength?

Are you willing to bear the weight?

Are you willing to become stronger?

Are you willing to stand up again?

Are you willing to fail greatly?

Are you willing to get back up?

Are you willing to then jump again?

Life asks many questions.
But it really comes down to: are you willing?

March 28

*I realized something on the ride. I realized if I wait until I'm not
scared to try new things, then I'll never get to try them at all.*
—Marie Sexton

This is your pep talk.

Get up
Get moving
Get to it
Do something
Do anything
Do what must be done
Make time
Make no excuses
Make up your mind

Try new
Try different
Try again
Be better
Be bigger
Be honest with yourself
Go hard
Go the distance
Go after what you want

Take a chance
Take one step
Take a risk
Trust the process
Trust the plan
Trust yourself
Live out loud
Live joyfully
Live your dream

You've just been pep-talked.

March 29

*We often lose ourselves to where we think we should be,
rather than celebrate where we already are.*
—*Chris Burkmenn*

Today is your day.

Celebrate you.

Live with arms wide open
Love with heart wide open
Dream with eyes wide open

Celebrate you.

Dance like everyone is watching
Shine like everyone is watching
Smile like everyone is watching

Celebrate you.

Sing from the heart
Speak from the heart
Listen from the heart

Celebrate you.

Do what makes you happy
Be with those who make you happy
Know you are allowed to be happy

Celebrate you.

Make time for you
Be completely you
Enjoy being you

Celebrate you.

Today is your day.

March 30

I am not what you see. I am what time and effort and interaction slowly unveil.
—*Richelle E. Goodrich*

I am unafraid
Of the silence
Of the darkness
Of the unknown

I am undeterred
By fears
By obstacles
By impossible

I am understanding
Of what must be done
Of where I want to be
Of who I am

I am unshaken
By yesterday's mistakes
By today's setbacks
By tomorrow's challenges

I am unapologetic
For my path
For my light
For my love

I am undefined
By thoughts of others
By words of others
By actions of others

I am unquestionably
Worthy
Beautiful
Loved

I am unwavering
In pursuit of my dreams
In the hope I hold
In my love for this life

I am undeniably me.

March 31

The truer you are to yourself, the greater your gifts will manifest themselves.
—Tiffany L. Jackson

Dear Life,

At times, you have been unbending.
Led me down a dead-end street I did not choose to travel.
And I remained open to the journey.

At times, you have been uncaring.
Left me discarded and lost in the silence.
And I remained humble and kind.

At times, you have been unfair.
Rules constantly changed and broken.
And I remained understanding.

At times, you have been unapologetic.
Wrongs committed, without an "I am sorry."
And I remained compassionate.

At times, you have been unforgiving.
Punished for that which was not my doing.
And I remained ever full of grace.

At times, you have been unfaithful to my dream.
So many nights stolen from me.
And I remained committed to it.

My life, you have been.

And I remained: simply me.

Love,

Me

April 1

The great beauty of life is its mystery, the inability to know what course our life will take, and diligently work to transmute into our final form based upon a lifetime of constant discovery and enterprising effort. Accepting the unknown and unknowable eliminates regret.
—Kilroy J. Oldster

I've known paralyzing fear. Whether real or fictitious.
Fear of loss. Fear of failure. Fear of loneliness.
Fear of the darkness.

I've known complete brokenness. For the loss was real.
My failure a truth. Left alone.
Came the darkness.

I've known love's good-bye. My heart felt its loss.
Failed to save it. Loneliness replaced it.
The darkness so deep.

Turned toward my fears. Sat with them.
Allowed them to pass through me.
And found once they were gone, I still remained.

Accepted my brokenness. Sat with it.
Allowed it to simply be.
And found all the pieces I would ever need still remained.

Understood love often leaves. Sat with it.
Allowed my heart to break open.
And found a place where love still remained.

It is the magic, the mystery, the truth of life.
What you need always remains.

April 2

There are some questions that shouldn't be asked until a
person is mature enough to appreciate the answers.
—Anne Bishop

I have questions. Life has answers. This is another life chat.

Me: Will you forgive me for my mistakes?
Life: I already have. Now, you must do the same.

Me: Can you tell me everything will be okay?
Life: Everything will be okay. But you must believe.

Me: When am I allowed to be happy again?
Life: The moment you finally decide. Happiness is simply waiting.

Me: Can you fix my brokenness?
Life: Each day, we will pick up the pieces. Together.

Me: Will you help me find my way?
Life: You are not lost. I led you here. This is right where you belong.

Me: What is in this place?
Life: Your answers. Your truth.

Me: May I ask yet another question?
Life: What could you have left to ask?

Me: Am I worthy of love?
Life: Dear child, you have always been.

April 3

Fallen man is not simply an imperfect creature who needs
improvement: he is a rebel who must lay down his arms.
—C. S. Lewis

The wars in my life raged.

And I was a combatant.

Fought my demons, my ghosts, and my past.

The wars in my life raged.

And I was a combatant.

Armed with indecision, fears, and despair.

The wars in my life raged.

And I was a combatant.

Arrows slung, stones cast, and shots fired.

The wars in my life raged.

And I was a combatant.

Suffered bruises, exit wounds, and bitter losses.

The wars in my life now over.

I am no longer a combatant.

For once I chose to lay down my arms, peace came upon me.

April 4

If you listen quietly enough life will whisper its secrets to you.
—Rasheed Ogunlaru

As I stood at the edge, fearing the leap, there came a whisper.

As I listened to the lies, accepting them as my truths, there came a whisper.

As I sat alone with my pain, willing to be broken, there came a whisper.

As I started to lose hope, letting go of that which I believe, there came a whisper.

As I began to close my heart, protecting it from damage, there came a whisper.

As I watched the darkness draw near, my brilliant light flickering, there came a whisper.

As I wandered aimlessly, feeling I should turn back, there came a whisper.

As I knelt in silent prayer, ready to surrender, there came a whisper.

"You are meant for more than this…"

April 5

When you wish someone joy, you wish them peace, love,
prosperity, happiness...all the good things.
—Maya Angelou

I wrote this for you, my friend.
There is something I want you to know.

In my next thought, you are gently on my mind.
May you realize you are not alone.

In my daily gratitude, you are counted as a blessing.
May you receive an abundance of blessings.

In my nightly prayer, your name is spoken.
May you know answered prayers.

In my beating heart, you are held ever so close.
May you feel my love.

In my hopes, you are wished joy, light, and love.
May your life hold all these.

There is something I want you to know.
You, my friend, are always in the best parts of me.

April 6

Your self-talk is the channel of behavior change.
—Gino Norris

I stopped listening to myself and started talking to myself.

I stopped listening to myself, for all I heard were words of doubt.
I started talking to myself, "Have faith."

I stopped listening to myself, for all I heard was the voice of fear.
I started talking to myself, "Do not be afraid."

I stopped listening to myself, for all I heard were echoes of regret.
I started talking myself, "Forgive yourself."

I stopped listening to myself, for all I heard were the whispers of cannot.
I started talking to myself: "Believe you will."

I started talking to myself.
And realized I was simply saying, "I love you."

April 7

Too often we underestimate the power of a touch, a smile, a kind word, a listening ear, an honest compliment, or the smallest act of caring, all of which have the potential to turn a life around.
—Leo Buscaglia

I come to you, hand extended
Open and empty
Yet asking for nothing
I simply wish to help you stand

I come to you seeking light
Warm and brilliant
Yet not my own
I simply hope to see you shine

I come to you on bended knees
Silent and bowed
Yet not needing help up
I simply am praying for you

I come to you as a friend
Caring and concerned
Yet knowing I have little to offer
I simply hope you know I'm here.

April 8

*The function of prayer is not to influence God, but rather
to change the nature of the one who prays.*
—Søren Kierkegaard

A morning prayer:

May I take the tools I have been given to build a better little corner of my world.

May I use the gifts I have been given to make the day brighter for another.

May I remain present enough to count the grand blessings in my life instead of adding up the minor problems that might arise.

May I patiently wait my turn as the day unfolds so others will not feel hurried or rushed.

May I not cross paths with another without leaving them in a better place for having shared time with me.

May I share the hope and love that exists in my heart so others may feel this in their day.

May I choose to walk forward this day, even if my steps are small, slow, clumsy, or heavy.

May I face the day full of wonder, willing to grow, accepting of what it brings, and ever grateful for the breaths it affords me.

May I do all this knowing I am cared about, watched over, and surrounded by and filled with love.

Amen.

April 9

*Ordinary people believe only in the possible. Extraordinary people
visualize not what is possible or probable, but rather what is impossible.
And by visualizing the impossible, they begin to see it as possible.*
—Cherie Carter-Scott

I used to believe in walls,
And they rose impassable before me.

I used to believe in limits,
And they kept me from my dreams.

I used to believe in fears,
And they grew to be larger than life.

I used to believe in the impossible,
And it read as my story's truth.

I used to believe in everything—
Except me.

I finally believe in me,
And the walls have crumbled before me.

I finally believe in me,
And there is no limit to what I can dream.

I finally believe in me,
And I am bigger than the sum of my fears.

I finally believe in me,
And impossible now reads I'm possible.

April 10

Heroes are made by the paths they choose, not the powers they are graced with.
—Brodi Ashton

I wondered, *what does it take to be a superhero?* Here's what I came up with.

How to be a superhero:

Forgive a wrong
Apologize when wrong

Be bigger than the hurt
Be big enough to let go the hurt

Never lose hope
If others do, be a source of hope

Spread your wings
Help another unfurl his or her wings

Make a difference
Accept others' differences

See your beauty
Hold the mirror so they see they're beautiful

Be kind
Stay kind when humankind seems unkind

Walk your talk
Listen more than you talk

Be great when no one is watching
Be humble when everyone is watching

Simply *love*
Unwavering, unconditionally...love.

April 11

In order to move forward, you will have to stumble along the way, but every falter in your stride just makes your next step even stronger.
—Lindsay Chamberlin

This is a story.

With every stride, I discovered my path

With every stride, I gained my strength

With every stride, I displayed my courage

With every stride, I embraced my peace

With every stride, I outdistanced my demons

With every stride, I established my pace

With every stride, I moved closer to my dream

With every stride, I further loosened my chains

With every stride, I vanquished my fears

With every stride, I surrendered my comfort

With every stride, I emboldened my warrior

With every stride, I took back my life

This is the moral of the story: every stride matters.

April 12

Freedom is not the absence of commitments, but the ability to choose—and commit myself to—what is best for me.
—Paulo Coelho

Some days I do not have it. But I give the best I have.
This is commitment.

Some days I do not feel like it. But I do it just the same.
This is discipline.

Some days I do not want it. But I still chase after it.
This is dedication.

Some days I do not believe it. But I continue to walk toward it.
This is trust.

Some days I do not know if I will achieve it. But I still reach for it.
This is desire.

Some days I question it. But I always find the answers.
This is faith.

Some days I feel like giving up on it. But I do not quit.
This is living.

April 13

Nothing can be more hurtful to your heart than betraying yourself.
—Roy T. Bennett

You can say I am clueless.
I do not live to impress anyone.
I am not consumed by another's thoughts of me.
They are none of my business.

You can say I am misguided.
I do not live in comparison to anyone.
The gifts of another do not diminish my own.
The light of another cannot dull my luster.

You can say I am arrogant.
I do not live to prove anything to anyone.
What someone believes about me matters not.
It does not impact what I believe.

You can say I am selfish.
I do not live to motivate anyone.
Motivation is highly overrated.
It is fickle, temperamental, and unreliable.
It is not what drives me.

You can say I am foolish.
I do not live to best anyone.
I am not chasing, or attempting to outdo, anyone.
Another's race does not concern me.

You can say what you will about me.
You simply cannot say I did not remain true to me.

April 14

I sold my soul for freedom. It's lonely but it's sweet.
—Melissa Etheridge

I am guilty. Of giving my all. Of sharing my gifts.
Of opening my heart.
My life's sentence: fulfillment.

I am guilty. Of never settling. Of never wavering.
Of never surrendering.
My life's sentence: possibilities.

I am guilty. Of letting go of the past. Of laying down my weapons.
Of forgiving wrongs done me.
My life's sentence: serenity.

I am guilty. Of trying. Of failing.
Of leaping.
My life's sentence: learning.

I am guilty. Of following my path. Of following my heart.
Of following my dreams.
My life's sentence: happiness.

I am guilty. Of wanting to give. Of wanting to believe.
Of wanting to make a difference.
My life's sentence: compassion.

I am guilty. Of loving so hard. Of trusting so much.
Of believing so deeply.
My life's sentence: vulnerability.

I am guilty. Of seeing with my heart. Of hoping with my heart.
Of dreaming with my heart.
My life's sentence: unwavering love.

I am guilty. But I am free.

April 15

I always wonder why birds stay in the same place
when they can fly anywhere on the earth.
—Harun Yahya

Life wants me to fly. This is another life chat.

Me: What is it that keeps me imprisoned in this cage I have built?
Life: It is what you see. When you can see only the bars, you cannot imagine life beyond them.

What is it that keeps me from moving toward the open door?
Life: Here is familiar. With familiarity comes comfort. Comfort leads to withering.

Me: What is it that causes me to cling to my perch?
Life: The need for safety. With safety there is no fear. One only lets go when one fears staying put.

Me: What is it that keeps my wings from being used?
Life: You do not believe. Without belief, the fall is the focus. When you focus on falling, you cannot soar.

Me: What is it that pulls me back down to earth?
Life: The burdens you travel with. Guilt. Shame. Regret. Hurt. As you release them, you will not be weighed down.

Me: What is it I now must do to truly fly?
Life: It is what it has always been. Simply grant yourself permission.

April 16

Wishes of one's old life wither and shrivel like old leaves if they are not replaced with new wishes when the world changes. And the world always changes.
—Catherynne M. Valente

I wish.
I wish you no longer wished you were someone different.
Who you are, in this moment, is enough. You are worthy.

I wish.
I wish you no longer compared yourself to another.
Who you are, as you are, is not lessened by another. You are enough.

I wish.
I wish you no longer viewed yourself as "just."
Who you are, all you are, cannot be minimized. You are significant.

I wish.
I wish you no longer allowed yourself to question your gifts.
Who you are, all you possess, is valuable. You are special.

I wish.
I wish you no longer worked from a model of deficit.
Who you are, what makes you complete, isn't about what you lack. You are whole.

I wish.
I wish you no longer accepted less than you deserve.
Who you are, within your heart, is your truth. You are loved.

This is my wish for you.

April 17

May you live every day of your life.
—Jonathan Swift

Life offers you a gift today.
A chance to dance.
A chance to dream.
A chance to become.
A chance to change.

Life will speak to you today.
The sound of laughter.
The sound of music.
The sound of joy.
The sound of love.

Life will move you today.
A step further.
A step closer.
A step forward.
A step beyond.

Life blesses you today.
With hope.
With faith.
With gifts.
With love.

Life accepts you today.
Where you are.
What you are.
Who you are.
As you are.

Life trusts you today.
To be strong.
To carry on.
To grow.
To believe.

Life is a friend today. Treat it as such.
Honor it.
Thank it.
Embrace it.
Love it.

April 18

I have a fear of living a surface kind of life; barely existing, barely touching or tasting anything. That's why you'll always see me giving my all or walking away—I'm too full of depth to dance in the middle of anything.
—Nikki Rowe

I am too full not to give. And so, I empty myself.
Giving of my light, my truth, my prayers, my love.

I am too full not to believe. And so, I trust.
Believing in my strength, my wings, my next step, my heart's voice.

I am too full not to search. And so, I wander.
Searching for unicorns, goose bumps, magic, holiness.

I am too full not to dream. And so, I imagine.
Dreaming of miracles, all the possibilities, happily ever after, an unwavering love.

I am too full not to dive into the deep end. And so, I launch myself.
Immersing myself in hope, light, laughter, love.

I am too full to sit it out. And so, I dance.
Taking life by the hand, leading it to the dance floor, pulling it close, and softly whispering, "May I have this dance?"

And oh, how I have danced.

April 19

Just knowing you're not alone is often enough to
kindle hope amid tragic circumstances.
—Richelle E. Goodrich

Perhaps you are hurting. Today, I write for you.

Dear Friend,

I know you sit with heartache.
Dull, constant, encompassing.
Know I will sit by your side.

I know you hold worry close.
It grows with time, it consumes time.
Know I will hold your hand.

I know you fear the darkness.
When the monsters come alive.
Know I will be there until the light arrives.

I know you feel an unspoken pain.
For scars etched upon you.
Know I will listen to your cries.

I know you are losing hope.
Waves of sorrow crash endlessly.
Know I will not abandon you.

I know you cannot hear my prayers.
But to the heavens I whisper your name.
Know I will again kneel for you tonight.

You are not alone.

Love,

Me

April 20

To love without need or without expectation of
restitution, that is how we ought to love.
—Criss Jami

If it is love, it is not given in expectation of what it shall receive.
It is unconditional. This is love.

If it is love, it is not given in bits and pieces.
It is immeasurable. This is love.

If it is love, it is not given simply in times of joy.
It is always. This is love.

If it is love, it is not given with a return policy.
It is nonrefundable. This is love.

If it is love, it is not given from a place of fear.
It is an act of courage. This is love.

If it is love, it is not given to quell a want.
It is to fulfill a need. This is love.

If it is love, it is not given at a cost.
It is priceless. This is love.

If it is love, it is not given just for now.
It is unwavering. This is love.

This is love.

April 21

Ultimately love is everything.
—M. Scott Peck

Where there is beauty,
bounty, blessings...there is love.

Where there is compromise,
communication, caring...there is love.

Where there is forgiveness,
faith, freedom...there is love.

Where there is gratitude,
giving, grace...there is love

Where there is hope, happiness,
home...there is love.

Where there is laughter, light,
listening...there is love.

Where there is magic, mystery,
majesty...there is love.

Where there is peace, promise,
patience...there is love.

Where there is trust,
time, thoughtfulness...there is love.

Where there is love...there is everything.

April 22

I have needs. This is another life chat.

Me: When will you offer what I need?
Life: I have offered you all you need.

Me: If this is true, how am I still in need?
Life: You did not accept what I offered.

Me: How can you say that?
Life: I offered you lessons in patience. But you said you were in a hurry.

Me: But I had places I needed to be.
Life: So I offered you a path. But you said it wasn't the way.

Me: But it looked too difficult.
Life: So I offered a chance to grow strong. But you said you were afraid.

Me: But I fear the unknown.
Life: So I offered you answers. But you said they were not your truth.

Me: But I was too broken to hear it.
Life: So I offered you love. But you said you were not ready.

Me: Will you offer me a second chance?
Life: Yes. I will again offer all you need.

Me: But when will this happen?
Life: When you have no more excuses.

April 23

The magic in this world seems to work in whispers and small kindnesses.
—Charles De Lint

When you yell, "Be strong!"
Please know: I am not weak.
For I am still moving forward.
But I have been buckled by the pain.

When you yell, "You can do this!"
Please know: I am uncertain.
For I have never been here before.
But I shall try and find a way.

When you yell, "Do not quit!"
Please know: I am merely resting.
For it is so very hard to breathe.
But I will not give up.

When you yell, "It will be okay!"
Please know: I am not okay.
For pieces of me have been broken.
But I am slowly in repair.

When you yell, "Get up!"
Please know: I am still falling.
For there was no net to catch me.
But in time, I shall rise again.

When you whisper, "I am here for you."
Please know: I hear you, my friend.
For it was your heart that spoke.
And it is what I was waiting to hear.

April 24

If you wish to be a warrior prepare to be broken, if you wish to be an explorer prepare to get lost, and if you wish to be a lover prepare to be both.
—Daniel Saint

I have done battle with my demons. All that which haunts me. My fears. My inadequacies. My echoes repeating, "You are not good enough."

I have fought to be heard. All my life. As words from the heart are often only whispered. But they are the only truth I have ever known.

I have competed with the me of yesterday. Looking only to better myself. An endless struggle for growth, worth, acceptance.

I wished to be a warrior. And I have been broken. So very many times.

I have searched. Wandering aimlessly toward a home I have never known. A place where I can finally take refuge from the storm.

I have explored. The deepest, darkest parts of me. The very corners that still frighten me. Looking for a light that will guide me.

I have looked. At this life through a different lens. And I have stood in awe of the colors, beauty, light it affords me.

I wished to be an explorer. And I have been lost. So very many times.

I have loved. Greatly. Deeply. Unwavering. Unconditionally. For my heart knows no other way.

I have loved. Fearlessly. Hopefully. Truthfully. Passionately. For my soul knows no other way.

I have loved. As if I have never been hurt. As if it were the only way to live. As if I have never loved before.

I wished to be a lover. And I have been broken and lost. So very many times.

The fight continues. The search goes on. The love does not end. It is all I know to do.

For I wished to be a warrior, an explorer, a lover.

April 25

Always bear in mind that your own resolution to succeed
is more important than any one thing.
—Abraham Lincoln

This is the secret to success.

Success:

Do the hard work

Become persistence

Expect late nights

Choose discipline over motivation

Learn from rejections

Act with courage

Accept criticism

Make changes

Take risks

Develop good habits

Seek innovation

Choose dedication over excuses

Make honesty your signature

Fearlessly live your passion

This is to know success.

April 26

Sitting silently beside a friend who is hurting may be the best gift we can give.
—Unknown

Dear Friend,

I know not how heavy your burden is this day. For I do not have this weight to bear. But I know my love will not collapse.

I know not how many tears will fall this day. For I do not have this pain to feel. But I know my love will not shrink.

I know not how the darkness falls upon you this day. For I do not see the shadows that walk with you. But I know my love will not fade away.

I know not how great the loneliness is this day. For I do not have this path to walk. But I know my love will not abandon you.

I know not how shaken you are this day. For I do not have the tremblings you know. But I know my love will not waver.

I know not the words to say this day. And so my love will sit silently beside you.

Hugs and prayers.

Love,

Me

April 27

At any given moment, you have the power to say
this is not how the story is going to end.
—M. H. S. Pourri

Dear Life,

You ripped out pages where once were written the words of my dreams. But I shall write another chapter.

You scribbled lies across pages that told my truth, hoping they would define me. But I shall write another chapter.

You highlighted pages that spoke of my flaws, falls, and failures. But I shall write another chapter.

You edited pages to the story I was writing, forever changing my tomorrows. But I shall write another chapter.

You erased pages that once held the letters of my love, as if it never existed at all. But I shall write another chapter.

You added pages I did not want to read, for this was not my ending. But I shall write another chapter.

And there is something you must know: as long as I am living, there will always be another chapter.

Love,

Me

April 28

Every new breath and day is on opportunity to do something,
a gift of life to make a difference in the world.
—*K. J. Kilton*

There is something inside of me.
A hunger. A thirst. An ache.

There is something inside of me.
Consumes me. Fuels me. Drives me.

There is something inside of me.
Growing. Burning. Unrelenting.

There is something inside of me.
Darkness. Brokenness. Emptiness.

There is something inside of me.
Uncontrolled. Untamed. Unapologetic.

There is something inside of me.
Raw. Fierce. Savage.

There is something inside of me.
Full of passion. Full of desire. Full of love.

There is something inside of me.
Magical. Beautiful. Wondrous.

There is something inside of me.
Fragile, yet unbreakable. Fleeting, yet eternal. Free, yet priceless.

There is something inside of me.
Granted unto me. And I, merely its vessel.

There is something inside of me.
It is now to me to allow it to burst forth.

There is something inside of me.
The very gift of life.

April 29

To find truth, one must traverse a dense fog.
—David Dweck

I began to view my journey differently
As a choice, as that of a warrior
And the fog slowly lifted

I began to view my failures differently
As learnings, as growth, as courage
And the fog slowly lifted

I began to view my purpose differently
As a mirror, as a lighthouse, as a giver
And the fog slowly lifted

I began to view myself differently
As worthy, as strong, as beautiful
And the fog slowly lifted

I began to view my life differently
As a gift, as a blessing, as a miracle
And the fog slowly lifted

And as the fog slowly lifted
Something began to come into view
It was my own amazing light

Nevermore shall I wander in the fog.

April 30

The real me isn't someone you see but someone you know.
—Richelle E. Goodrich

I have been called foolish
For simply believing
In the impossible
In dreams I chase
In love unwavering

I have been called stubborn
For simply believing
That I might
That I can
That I will

I have been called selfish
For simply believing
I am deserving of more
I am a priority
I am worthy

I have been called crazy
For simply believing
Hope is stronger than fear
Light trumps darkness
Love conquers hate

I have been called arrogant
For simply believing
In my dreams
In my gifts
In my *self*

This is the moral of the story: I have been called many names to which I do not respond. I simply believe they must not know me.

May 1

If a man is to shed the light of the sun upon other men,
he must first of all have it within himself.
—Romain Rolland

The light in you
It is hope
Let it shine

The light in you
It is faith
Let it lead you

The light in you
It is courage
Let it wash over you

The light in you
It is peace
Let it calm you

The light in you
It is forgiveness
Let it heal you

The light in you
It is strength
Let it move you

The light in you
It is love
Let it become you

The light in you
It is you
And *you* are beautiful.

May 2

Believing there is a bridge from where you are to where you want
to go is 99% of the battle. The other 1% is to cross it.
—*Richie Norton*

This, my lot in life
I am not always where I want to be
Yet I always know I will get there
Because I believe

This, my lot in life
I have heard prayers go unanswered
Yet I always listen
Because I believe

This, my lot in life
I do not have everything I want
Yet I always have what I need
Because I believe

This, my lot in life
I have stumbled in the darkness
Yet I always find the light
Because I believe

This, my lot in life
I have not reached the mountaintop
Yet I always keep climbing
Because I believe

This, my lot in life
I have seen love as it walks away
Yet I always trust it to return
Because I believe

This, my lot in life
I have a lot in my life
Simply
Because I believe.

May 3

Failure is a bruise, not a tattoo.
—Jon Sinclair

This not easy to craft, for it speaks of my failures. Things I often wish others did not know.

Throughout my life, I have failed. At things small. At things grand. At so many, many things.

When I was eleven, I failed to get out of the first round of the spelling bee.

When I was thirteen, I failed to drive in the winning run to advance my team to the Little League World Series.

When I was seventeen, I failed to ask the girl I had a crush on to the homecoming dance.

When I was twenty-one, I failed three classes and was placed on academic probation.

When I was twenty-four, I failed to pass my college internship.

When I was twenty-eight, I failed to know what I wanted to do with my life.

When I was thirty, I failed to win a prestigious, national first-year-teacher award.

When I was thirty-eight, I failed at my marriage.

When I was forty, I failed to win more than one game and was fired as head basketball coach.

When I was forty-five, I failed to win more than two games and was fired as a baseball coach.

When I was forty-nine, I failed at love once again.

When I was fifty-four, I failed to run 2,015 miles in 2015.

When I was fifty-five, I failed to be the man she could or wanted to love.

Throughout my life, I have failed. At things small. At things grand. At so many, many things. And I am sure I shall fail again.

Yet, my life will not be defined by my failures. For I will not allow my failures to be the end of the story I am writing for myself.

They have been lessons learned, obstacles overcome, strengths gained, challenges accepted, memories made, bruises earned, chapters fully lived.

And from all of them, I am becoming the success I always believed I could be.

May 4

We are, largely, who we remember ourselves to be
—Holly Black

Dear Friend,

Even during your darkest hours, you have a path. You simply must remember your light. It is faith.

Even during your winter's storms, you have a safe harbor. You simply must remember your anchor. It is forgiveness.

Even during your weakest moments, you have enough strength. You simply must remember your power. It is trust.

Even during your chaos, you have peace. You simply must remember your calm. It is acceptance.

Even during your struggles, you have a way through. You simply must remember your courage. It is hope.

Even during your losses, you have enough. You simply must remember your abundance. It is gratitude.

Even during your brokenness, you have wholeness. You simply must remember your complete story. It is love.

You simply must remember.

Love,

Me

May 5

Whatever it takes to find the real you, don't be daunted
if the rest of the world looks on in shock.
—Stephen Richards

I found myself upon my knees.
Brought there by burdens too heavy to bear.
And so I did the only thing I knew.
I prayed for strength to rise again.

I found myself filled with doubt.
Brought there by questions I had no answers for.
And so I did the only thing I knew.
I searched for my heart's truths.

I found myself surrounded by darkness.
Brought there by the shadows of my fears.
And so I did the only thing I knew.
I allowed my courage to shine.

I found myself broken.
Brought there by the harshness of this life's trials.
And so I did the only thing I knew.
I stitched together the very best parts of me.

I found myself alone.
Brought there by love's departure.
And so I did the only thing I knew.
I took comfort in the grace of my own loving company.

Life has challenged me.
And so I did the only thing I knew.
I found myself.

May 6

Go after what gives you goosebumps.
—Tara Stiles

Hey you....

This is your life speaking. Your one, amazing, beautiful, audacious life.

This is just a gentle reminder.

I have hopes for you.

I hope you never settle. For comfortable. For mediocre. For easy. For less than you deserve.

I hope for you breathlessness. Moments that require you to come up for air. Moments that leave you in awe. Moments that make your heart beat faster. Moments that add up to an amazing life.

I hope you never back away from the sexy dream that calls your name. I hope you pull it close. Give it a long, soft, wet kiss. And never, ever let it go.

I hope you love and are loved. In a way that sets you free. In a crazy, head-over-feet-I'm-so-deeply-in-love-with-you kind of way. In a not just now kind of love, but an always kind of love.

I hope for you goose bumps. From the rush, the fear, the not knowing. From the touch, the whisper, the kiss. From the leap of faith, the soaring, the free falling.

I have hopes for you. Go get your goose bumps.

Love,

Your one, amazing, beautiful, audacious life

May 7

It is our wounds that create in us a desire to reach for miracles.
The fulfillment of such miracles depends on whether we let our
wounds pull us down or lift us up toward our dreams.
—Jocelyn Soriano

It is not that I have never known tears, it is that I have so much to smile about.

It is not that I have never been hurt, it is that I possess the healing power of forgiveness.

It is not that I have never faced hardships, it is that I refuse to be defined by them.

It is not that I have never gotten lost along the way, it is that I have faith I will always find my way.

It is not that I have never failed, it is that I will not let failure be my finish line.

It is not that I have never felt fear, it is that I understand my fears do not control me.

It is not that I have never been broken, it is that I am greater than the sum of my pieces.

It is not that I have a perfect life, it is that I have been afforded but one earthly life to make the most of.

May 8

Our stresses, anxieties, pains, and problems arise because we do not
see the world, others, or even ourselves as worthy of love.
—Prem Prakash

Dear Friend,

There are words I wish to speak to you, but I wonder if you will go beyond hearing, and truly listen to them? Will you quiet the voices and noise that you allow to be the soundtrack of your life?

You are not "useless." For I need you. I need your light and laughter, your gifts and presence. Without them, my day is a little less bright, a little less warm, a little less. You are valuable.

You are not "less than." For I see the great in you. It takes greatness to make a difference. To change the world, your world. To live and love in a world wanting to steal your value. You are amazing.

You are not "lazy." For I see the hard work you are doing. How you are changing your life. How you are doing the difficult work of taking care of you. How you are getting stronger. You are a dream chaser.

You are not "ugly." For I see the beauty in you. In your smile when you greet me. In your eyes when you speak of all you love. In your heart when you give to those around you. You are beautiful.

You are not "worthless." Oh, my dear sweet child, you are so very worthy. Of joy and peace and hope and dreams and love. Your worth is not defined by the words of others, but by how you live your life. You are worthy.

I shall hold you in my thoughts and prayers. And I hope you shall hold these words as your truth.

Love,

Me

May 9

They say a person needs just three things to be truly happy in this world:
someone to love, something to do, and something to hope for.
—Tom Bodett

I ran
Through lies told to my heart
Hoping to make them true

I ran
Down many broken roads
Hoping they would lead me home

I ran
To the middle of nowhere
Hoping to find myself again

I ran
Despite an excruciating pain
Hoping not to be shattered

I ran
As the nightmare played out
Hoping it was all just a dream

I ran
Echoes of failure calling my name
Hoping to silence the screams

I ran
Watching as love walked away
Hoping for its return

I run
Hoping.

May 10

*Mature love is composed and sustaining; a celebration
of commitment, companionship, and trust.*
—H. Jackson Brown, Jr.

It was not love that cheated

It was not love that lied

It was not love that stole something

It was not love that made you feel fear

It was not love that took the easy way out

It was not love that walked away

It was not love that broke you

That was not love.

It is love that forgives

It is love that finds a way to trust again

It is love that offers everything

It is love that makes you feel goose bumps

It is love that endures the difficult

It is love that remains unwavering

It is love that holds you together

This is love.

May 11

I don't think that we're meant to understand it all the time.
I think that sometimes we just have to have faith.
—Nicholas Sparks

Strength.

It is found in the small, simple acts of today.
When you try again.
When you do one more than you thought you could.
Simply in the rising.
Search there. You shall find your strength.

Faith.

It is kept in the small, simple acts of today.
When you fall to your knees.
When you do not give up.
Simply in the moving forward.
That you struggle but do not quit, this is faith.

Forgiveness.

It exists in the small, simple acts of today.
When you give yourself permission to be okay.
When you whisper to yourself, "I love you."
Simply in the letting go.
And in the forgiveness, you shall find your way.

Strength. Faith. Forgiveness.

Found in the small, simple acts of today.

May 12

Your journey inspires me
With each step you take
I believe I will find my finish

Your light inspires me
When you illuminate the path
I can see the direction I must go

Your strength inspires me
When you refuse to bow
I know I can endure my struggles

Your courage inspires me
When you show you're brave
I no longer let fear be my truth

Your fire inspires me
When you stand amid the flames
I learn to accept the burn

Your story inspires me
When I read of how far you have come
I trust this is not where my story ends

You inspire me
When you show up as you
I am made better for it.

May 13

Soon, when all is well, you're going to look back on this period
of your life and be so glad that you never gave up.
—Brittany Burgunder

It is not that I do not grow weary
When you have a mind that never sleeps
The tired settles in like an old friend

It is not that I do not often hurt
When you exist as a gentle soul
The pain of others is ever present

It is not that I do not know failure
When you dream that beyond your limits
The impossible often feels a truth

It is not that I am unafraid
When you dare go always to the ledge
The fear crawls upon you as a second skin

It is not that I have not been broken
When you live from a place of love
The world has easy access to your heart

It is simply this. I never learned to quit.

May 14

To move forward, you must first take a step.
—Chase S. M. Neill

I watch as you silently struggle
No words as you move forward
But with each new step
I hear you say, "I can."

I watch as you silently fight
No words as you face the demons
But with each new battle
I hear you say, "I can."

I watch as you silently climb
No words as you make the ascent
But with each new mountain
I hear you say, "I can."

I watch as you silently fall
No words as you are buckled
But with each new rising
I hear you say, "I can."

I watch as you silently break
No words as you are wounded
But with each new scar
I hear you say, "I can."

I watch as you silently grow
No words as you stretch
But with each new reach
I hear you say, "I can."

I watch as you silently succeed
No words as you achieve
But with each new victory
I hear you say, "I am."

May 15

I am still learning
Through the trials and stumbles
Through the missteps and mistakes
I am still learning

I am still trying
Despite the bruises and scars
Despite the setbacks and unknowns
I am still trying

I am still fighting
For my strength to be realized
For my place to stand
I am still fighting

I am still becoming
The me I hope to be
The me I am worthy of
I am still becoming

I am still growing
Beyond the limits of my fear
Beyond the comfort of my excuses
I am still growing

I am still dreaming
Of the truths I hold closest
Of one day coming home
I am still dreaming

I am still unwavering
In the love I have to offer
In the love I hope to know
I am still unwavering

I am. Still.

May 16

Self-discipline is the ability to organize your behavior
over time in the service of specific goals.
—Nathaniel Branden

I lean on you to get me there. Discipline.

I believe in you to get me there. Self-worth.

I look to you to get me there. Dreams.

I call on you to get me there. Faith.

I trust in you to get me there. Purpose.

I keep you to get me there. Promise.

I need you to get me there. Love.

I will get there. For I have you.

May 17

*It's a strange thing to discover and to believe that you are loved when you
know that there is nothing in you for anybody but a parent or a God to love.*
—Graham Greene

Dear Friend,

There are things I hope you know.

You are not alone. I cannot walk this difficult path for you. This is your journey, but
I will walk beside you as you make your way along.

You are cared about. I cannot take care of you. This is your work to do, but I will not
turn away should the work begin to break you.

You are held in prayer. I whisper your name to the heavens every night when I fall to
my knees. And I pray for your strength and grace.

You are in my thoughts. I keep you held closely, so you are never far away. I may not
be with you, yet you are only a thought away.

You are allowed all the feelings. Joy and despair, guilt and acceptance, anger and love,
pain and happiness. There is no right or wrong for how you feel.

You owe nothing. This is your journey. You need not apologize or prove anything. To
anyone. Do what serves your good.

You are going to find a way. Somehow. You will come through all you are facing. It
may take time. You may struggle. You may not feel okay. But you will arrive.

You are loved. Above all else, hold on to this knowing. Allow yourself to feel the love that surrounds you and welcomes you home. It is unwavering.

Love,

Me

May 18

It is when we are completely fulfilled and want for
nothing more that we are given everything.
—Kate McGahan

I have nothing but this steady resolve
Ever willing to take but one more step
Therefore, success remains possible.

I have nothing but this endless gratitude
Ever thankful for all my blessings
Therefore, happiness remains possible.

I have nothing but this constant belief
Ever trusting my wings are developing
Therefore, growth remains possible.

I have nothing but this quiet confidence
Ever humble yet aware of my gifts
Therefore, the dream remains possible.

I have nothing but this gentle heart
Ever following where it shall lead
Therefore, love remains possible.

I have nothing but this unwavering hope
Ever believing in what is still unseen
Therefore, everything remains possible.

I have nothing, but yet I have everything.

May 19

There is no worth in a candle without a flame, and we only add the flame when there is darkness. Without darkness, there would be no need for warriors and angels. Warriors are not made because the whole world is happy and angels were not formed because there are no demons. Be of worth, have a flame.
—C. JoyBell C.

When comes the darkness.

Light a flame.
For it shall illuminate the darkness.

When comes the darkness.

Become a lighthouse.
For it shall lead many out of the darkness.

When comes the darkness.

Look toward the sun.
For it scatters the darkness.

When comes the darkness.

Share your light.
For it conquers the darkness.

When comes the darkness.

Remember the light.
And darkness can never vanquish it.

May 20

You want help? Ask for help. You want love? Ask for love. If you want anything from the universe, anything from yourself, you must first ask.
—*Kamand Kojouri*

I'm not needing to be cared for.

I'm wanting to be cared about. And it really doesn't take much. Listen to my fears. Honor my journey. Allow me my passions. Support my dreams.

I'm not needing to be the only priority.

I'm wanting to be a priority. Invest time in me. Uninterrupted time. Spend time with me. Doing nothing. Doing everything. Share time with me. Making memories.

I'm not needing to be saved.

I'm wanting to be allowed to save myself. Do not fear my brokenness. I am in repair. Do not give up on me. Allow me to start over. As many times as it takes. Do not provide my answers. Be okay with my questions.

I'm not needing to be loved unconditionally.

I'm wanting to be loved unwaveringly. Feel free to put conditions on love that center on honesty, faithfulness, communication, commitment. But love me through all my faults and flaws, missteps and mistakes.

I am not needing. I am wanting.

May 21

No one ever excused his way to success.
—*Dave Del Dotto*

I am coming to realize:

1. There are no reasons I cannot succeed. Only excuses I have allowed myself to believe.

2. There are no dreams beyond my grasp. Only excuses I continue to desperately cling to.

3. There are no paths I am unable to travel. Only excuses I have used as roadblocks.

4. There are no truths I am forbidden to speak. Only excuses that keep me silent.

5. There are no fears greater than my belief. Only excuses that grow larger for relying on them

6. There are no limits to how high I can soar. Only excuses I accept to keep myself

I am coming to realize, only excuses stand in my way. No fear. No limits. No excuses.

May 22

But knowing about someone doesn't equate to knowing them.
—Kasie West

You see the path I now stand upon.
You know not what led me to arrive in this place or where I go from here.
Please be gentle when offering directions.

You see the shape I have now taken.
You know not the forces that conspired to mold me.
Please be gentle as you ask me to bend for you.

You see the scars I now bear.
You know not the pain suffered as they were inflicted upon me.
Please be gentle not to open these wounds.

You see the broken remnants now of a life I once knew.
You know not what shattered me.
Please be gentle with my remaining pieces.

You see the blank page I am now preparing to write upon.
You know not the words that shall be written.
Please be gentle not to craft your own conclusion.

You see the me of today.
But you do not know me.
So please, be gentle.

May 23

What you choose also chooses you.
—Kamand Kojouri

In a world saying, "Look at me."

Choose to be a mirror.

Choose to shine a light on others.

Choose to reflect beauty.

In a world asking, "What about me?"

Choose to ask, "What can I offer?"

Choose to ask, "Have I served another?"

Choose to ask, "How can I make a difference?"

In a world screaming, "Pay attention to me!"

Choose to quietly go about the business of being excellent.

Choose to silently pray for those in greater need.

Choose to let your quiet acts of kindness speak for you.

In a world whispering, "Hope is lost."

Choose to hope.

Choose to believe.

Choose to love.

May 24

How would your life be different if...You stopped allowing other people to dilute or poison your day with their words or opinions? Let today be the day...You stand strong in the truth of your beauty and journey through your day without attachment to the validation of others.
—Steve Maraboli

They may whisper,
"You cannot do this."
It does not make it so.

They may scream,
"You are not worthy."
It does not make it so.

They may speak without words,
"You do not belong."
It does not make it so.

They make echo your past:
"You will not succeed."
It does not make it so.

They may question you:
"Do you really believe you can fly?"
It does not make it so.

The only words you need hear:
I can. I am. I do. I will. I believe.
Now make it so.

May 25

To be one's self, and unafraid whether right or wrong, is more admirable than the easy cowardice of surrender to conformity.
—Irving Wallace

Quietly afraid
Quietly struggling
Quietly praying
I am quietly me

Hopefully searching
Hopefully dancing
Hopefully dreaming
I am hopefully me

Amazingly fragile
Amazingly strong
Amazingly blessed
I am amazingly me

Simply complex
Simply misunderstood
Simply learning
I am simply me

Perfectly flawed
Perfectly imperfect
Perfectly enough
I am perfectly me

Beautifully broken
Beautifully scarred
Beautifully lost
I am beautifully me

Always humble
Always kind
Always worthy
I am always me

That's just me. Being me.

May 26

Whatever you are physically...male or female, strong or weak, ill or healthy—all those things matter less than what your heart contains. If you have the soul of a warrior, you are a warrior. All those other things, they are the glass that contains the lamp, but you are the light inside.
—Cassandra Clare

There is a warrior in me
Never to surrender
There is a poet in me
Laying down my weapons

There is a warrior in me
Standing amid the flames
There is a poet in me
Lost among the ashes

There is a warrior in me
Silent in my resolve
There is a poet in me
Whispers from my heart

There is a warrior in me
A heart still beating
There is a poet in me
A heart broken so many times

There is a warrior in me
Taking the long way home
There is a poet in me
A soul forever searching

There is a warrior in me
Created from this hard life
There is a poet in me
Born to tell my story.

May 27

Always listen to your HEART. The wisdom of your heart is the connection to your authentic power—the true home of your spirit.
—Angie Karan

When the weight you carry serves to bring you down, let it go.

When the weight you carry serves to make you stronger, take it with you.

When the knee you take serves to make you bow before your fears, get back up.

When the knee you take serves to let you count your blessings, stay a moment longer.

When the effort you are investing is time wasted, turn your attention elsewhere.

When the effort you are investing serves your good, give all you have.

When the steps you are taking lead you in the wrong direction, find a new path.

When the steps you are taking lead you forward, keep moving.

When you don't know the difference, simply listen to the whisper in your heart.

It will let you know when.

May 28

Never in the field of human conflict was so much owed by so many to so few.
—*Winston S. Churchill*

If letters could reach heaven...

This is an open letter.

Dear fallen heroes,

You did not know me, and yet you stood for me. I can but kneel in remembrance and prayer for you.

You did not know me, and yet you fought for me. I am grateful for the peace you afforded me.

You did not know me, and yet you faced fear for me. I am less afraid knowing you were there protecting me.

You did not know me, and yet you sacrificed for me. I shall live to be worthy of the gifts you unselfishly gave me.

You did not know me, and yet you laid down your life for me. I will not take for granted the freedom I have to live my life.

You did not know me, and yet you put me before your family and yourself. I cannot repay you for this greatest of loves.

I did not know you. And yet, you are my brothers and my sisters. I will remember you always.

Love,

A free and grateful American

May 29

Essentially there are two actions in life: Performance and excuses.
Make a decision as to which you will accept from yourself.
—Steven Brown

I have my excuses.
As If skin, no matter how many times I shed them, they return to cover me.

I have my excuses.
As if fears, no matter how many times I face them, they still can paralyze me.

I have my excuses.
As if storytellers, no matter how many times I silence them, they still whisper to me.

I have my excuses.
As if gatekeepers, no matter how many times I pass them by, they want proof I am worthy to move on.

I have my excuses.
As if a favorite blanket, no matter how many times I believe I have outgrown them, they can still provide me comfort.

I have my excuses.
As if songs, no matter how many times I want to tune them out, they are stuck playing over and over in my head.

I have my excuses.
What matters is whether I use them.

As if.

May 30

One person can make a difference. In fact, it's not only possible
for one person to make a difference, it's essential that one person
makes a difference. And believe it or not, that person is you.
—Bob Riley

There is so much I wish I could make different.

This is another life chat.

Me: There is so much anger.
Life: Your gentleness is needed.

Me: A single word cannot calm the world.
Life: It doesn't need to. It need simply be heard by another.

Me: There is so much darkness.
Life: Your candle is needed.

Me: A single candle cannot light the world.
Life: It doesn't need to. It need simply light another's candle.

Me: There is so much brokenness.
Life: Your healing is needed.

Me: A single touch cannot heal the world.
Life: It doesn't need to. It need simply be felt by another.

Me: There is so much hatred.
Life: Your love is needed.

Me: A single act of love cannot change the world.
Life: It doesn't need to. It need simply change another's world.

Me: Are you saying I can make a difference?
Life: You need to.

May 31

Don't compromise yourself—you're all you have.
—John Grisham

Today.

I will simply be grateful. For everything.

I will simply be open. To the possibility.

I will simply be gentle. In word and action.

I will simply be present. Accepting of now.

I will simply be aware. Of life's beauty.

I will simply be happy. By choice.

I will simply be still. Allowing peace.

I will simply be brave. Setting fear aside.

I will simply be strength. Personified.

I will simply be honest. With myself.

I will simply be complete. All is within me.

I will simply be love. For I am needed.

Today.

I will simply be. Me.

June 1

It's the possibility that keeps me going, not the guarantee.
—Nicholas Sparks

I am not guaranteed that I will not get lost along the way.
But I am ever worthy of being allowed to wander where my heart may lead.

I am not guaranteed that I will never know failure.
But I am ever worthy of the right to begin again.

I am not guaranteed that I won't make grand mistakes.
But I am ever worthy of forgiveness.

I am not guaranteed that all my dreams shall come true.
But I am ever worthy of the dreams I hold within me.

I am not guaranteed that I will know a happily ever after.
But I am ever worthy of a happiness I alone create.

I am not guaranteed that love will find its way to me.
But I am ever worthy of an unwavering love.

I am not guaranteed. But I am ever worthy.

June 2

I'm the cover of a book, whose pages are still being written.
—Richard L. Ratliff

When you speak of my struggles,
Be sure to tell of how I never gave up.

When you speak of my stumbles,
Be sure to tell of the burdens I bore.

When you speak of my falls,
Be sure to tell of all my risings.

When you speak of my pain,
Be sure to tell of how much I endured.

When you speak of my failures,
Be sure to tell of the size of my dreams.

When you speak of my fears,
Be sure to tell of the courage I summoned.

When you speak of my scars,
Be sure to tell of the warrior I became.

When you speak of my brokenness,
Be sure to tell of how deeply I loved.

When you speak of me,
Be sure to tell my entire story.

June 3

*I can't cure anyone. I can't guarantee they will heal. I can only
tell them my story, remind them that they are not alone in
their journey and offer a glimmer of hope for healing.*
—Sharon E. Rainey

I listened as you told of your struggle.

And I spoke not a word.

There is a reason for my silence.

For there are things I cannot tell you.

I cannot tell you, "This will be easy." For I know not the struggle you face. But I know of your strength.

I cannot tell you, "If I can do this, so can you." For I know not the path you walk. But I know of your spirit.

I cannot tell you, "Do not be afraid." For I know not the fears you face. But I know of your courage.

I cannot tell you, "Everything will be okay." For I know not what breaks you. But I know of your faith.

I cannot tell you, "This too shall pass." For I know not what awaits you. But I know of your capacity to endure.

But when I speak, I only hope you can hear.

And this is what I will say to you: "I believe in your strength and am amazed by your spirit. Your courage and faith inspire me. I trust you shall endure."

June 4

We are more than the bodies we inhabit. They're little more than clothes, and yet we judge so much by them.
—Michael J. Sullivan

It is my body
Until you have lived in my skin
Until you have known my struggles
Until you have felt what it is to be me
You do not get to speak of it

It is my body
Unless your words are welcomed
Unless your words bring no shame
Unless your words conceal no weapons
You do not get to speak of it

It is my body
Until you wear my scars
Until you see beyond my flaws
Until you possess no judgments
You do not get to speak of it

It is my body
Unless you believe in me
Unless you love me
Unless you are me
You do not get to speak of it

It is my body.
You do not get to speak of it.

June 5

This is a story.

Do not expect failure to be the end of the story.

It is often the place from which the story can truly begin.

Do not expect failure to be a permanent mark upon you.

It is often that which wipes the slate clean.

Do not expect failure to be the chain locking you to the past.

It is often the key that opens the door to your future.

Do not expect failure to be the force that cripples you.

It is often the power to propel you forward.

Do not expect failure to be the excuse for not trying once more.

It is often the reason you should try again.

Do not expect failure to shatter you.

It is often that which serves to put you back together again.

This is the moral of the story: Do not expect failure. It is often the surest way to succeed.

June 6

*Believe in your infinite potential. Your only limitations
are those you impose upon yourself.*
—Roy Bennett

What becomes your limit?

Because it will be difficult?
Because another thought it impossible?

What becomes your limit?

Because you tried once or twice before?
Because you previously failed?

What becomes your limit?

Because you are afraid?
Because you do not know the answer?

What becomes your limit?

Because it may hurt?
Because it may even break you a little?

What becomes your limit?

Because it may require change?
Because it may highlight weaknesses?

What becomes your limit?

Because the road is long?
Because you see no ending in sight?

What becomes your limit, becomes your greatest excuse.

No excuses. Be limitless.

June 7

Never underestimate the difference YOU can make in the lives of others. Step forward, reach out and help. This week reach to someone that might need a lift.
—Pablo

This is a story.

Of you
I am in awe
I am amazed
I am inspired

By you
I am driven
I am motivated
I am pushed

Knowing you
I am included
I am changed
I am humbled

With you
I am lifted up
I am becoming more
I am made better

Because of you
I am redefining me
I am rethinking possible
I am realizing my gifts

This is the moral of the story: you make a difference to me.

June 8

I climbed a mountain, my friend.

And in the approaching distance, another rises before me.

And I go forth as I always do.

Head up, filled with faith, trusting in my strength, quietly confident I shall find a way.

I climbed a mountain, my friend.

And in the approaching distance, another rises before me. Higher. More difficult.

And still, I go forth as I always do.

Armed with prayer, willing to fail, unafraid of the fall.

I climbed a mountain, my friend.

And in the approaching distance, another rises before me. The summit a place I have never been.

And still, I go forth as I always do.

Eyes on the very next step, listening to my heart, sure of the destination.

I climbed a mountain, my friend.

And, I shall climb this one too.

June 9

Sometimes your joy is the source of your smile, but sometimes
your smile can be the source of your joy.
—Thich Nhat Hanh

Smile.

For it welcomes another.

And without a sound it speaks, "I mean you no harm."

Smile.

For it lets the light in.

And without a sound it speaks, "Today, I choose to be okay."

Laugh.

For it is music without words.

And it allows others to dance with you.

Laugh.

For it is love without words.

And it allows others the freedom to sing their own song.

Express joy.

For it is the signature of your heart.

And from there, you can write a beautiful beginning.

Express joy.

For it is the signature of your life.

And from there, you can write the dreams you dream.

Things to do: Smile. Laugh. Express joy.

June 10

The best way to find anything is to look with an opened mind.
—Richard Diaz

Do not mistake my silence as meaning I have nothing important to say.

You see, I simply want my actions to speak more clearly.

Do not mistake my discipline as meaning I have too narrow a vision.

You see, I imagine many dreams unfolding before me, and I must commit to them.

Do not mistake my focus as meaning I am antisocial.

You see, I am fully aware of your presence, and it inspires me forward; I simply crave the quiet.

Do not mistake my search for the light as meaning I crave the spotlight.

You see, I prefer to go unseen amid the crowd, just no longer amid the darkness.

Do not mistake my stare as meaning I am lost, looking for something out there.

You see, I am seeking something that exists within me.

Do not mistake my quiet confidence as meaning I think I am a superhero.

You see, I simply believe I am powerful enough to save myself.

You see me. But you may be mistaken as to who I am. Do not be afraid to change your filter.

June 11

Those who overcome great challenges will be changed, and often in unexpected ways. For our struggles enter our lives as unwelcome guests, but they bring valuable gifts. And once the pain subsides, the gifts remain. These gifts are life's true treasures, bought at great price, but cannot be acquired in any other way.
—Steve Goodier

There will be times when it will not be easy.

When the challenge set before you seems to demand too much.

There will be times when it will not be easy.

When the burden set upon you seems too great to bear.

There will be times when it will not be easy.

When the road stretching out ahead of you seems too long to travel.

There will be times when it will not be easy.

When the question posed to you seems too difficult to answer.

There will be times when it will not be easy.

When the task given you seems to break you into too many pieces.

There will be times when it will not be easy.

When the fears that grip you seem too real to overcome.

There will be times when it will not be easy.

When the scale of the dream seems too immense to be realized.

There will be times when it will not be easy.

And then you realize, you did not come here for easy.

Accept the challenge. Bear the weight. Start down the road. Seek your answers. Pick up the pieces. Let go of the fear. Chase the dream.

June 12

Without leaps of imagination or dreaming, we lose the excitement
of possibilities. Dreaming, after all is a form of planning.
—*Gloria Steinem*

When it comes to dreaming, dream of all that beyond your limits and imagination.

When it comes to dreaming, dream of all that which calls to your heart and soul.

When it comes to dreaming, dream of all that fills your spirit and sets you to flying.

When it comes to dreaming, dream of all that outside the boundaries of what yesterday held.

When it comes to dreaming, dream of all that which brings you goose bumps.

When it comes to dreaming, dream of all that moves you to dance and sing and smile and shine.

When it comes to dreaming, dream of all that allows you to grow and become and emerge as your authentic self.

When it comes to dreaming, dream of all that grants you permission to fulfill your promises.

When it comes to dreaming, live your dream.

June 13

I thought I was stronger than a word, but I just discovered that having to say goodbye to you is by far the hardest thing I've ever had to do.
—*Colleen Hoover*

I have a difficult time saying good-bye. A difficult time letting go.

For there were moments of light and laughter and love and pure joy.

And I wonder, shall I know them once more?

I have a difficult time saying good-bye. A difficult time turning the page.

For there was a beautiful story being written.

And I wonder, were there pages I left empty?

I have a difficult time saying good-bye. A difficult time moving forward.

For there was a feeling as if I had finally arrived, as if I was finally home.

And I wonder, when shall I be made to wander no more?

I have a difficult time saying good-bye.

And so, for now, I shall simply say, "See you soon."

For I will return. When your flowers are once again in full bloom. When spring returns to your shores. When you are ready to once more welcome me home.

For you remain the dream.

June 14

In the pursuit of dreams, your unshakable commitment is the only force more powerful than your thoughts, feelings and beliefs. Commitment will pull you toward the fulfilment of your idea even when you doubt yourself.
—Dragos Bratasanu

Stay strong
Stay humble
Stay focused
Stay disciplined
Chase the dream

Keep your head up
Keep your worries few
Keep your excuses fewer
Keep your eyes forward
Chase the dream

Remember who you are
Remember what you want
Remember setbacks happen
Remember the journey is long

Chase the dream

Remain patient
Remain confident
Remain hope-filled
Remain open to the lessons
Chase the dream

Be yourself always
Be faithful to the goal
Be a model of consistency
Be intentional in your choices
Chase the dream

Celebrate you
Celebrate living
Celebrate each step
Celebrate the journey
Chase the dream

Things to do: chase your dreams.

June 15

Any moment which is not captured is lost in the events of time.
—Lailah Gifty Akita

Simply trust
Simply hope
Simply believe
Simply dream
Capture the moment

Know laughter
Know joy
Know happiness
Know peace
Capture the moment

Make time
Make memories
Make room for silly
Make someone's day
Capture the moment

Live humbly
Live gently
Live your dream
Live your love
Capture the moment

Let down your guard
Let yourself show
Let love in
Let love out
Capture the moment

Things to do: capture your moments.

June 16

Cultivate the habit of being grateful for every good thing that comes to you, and to give thanks continuously. And because all things have contributed to your advancement, you should include all things in your gratitude.
—Ralph Waldo Emerson

This is a story.

On the way to a dream, there were times I felt so very lost.

Yet, I found the courage to whisper, "Thank you for showing me a new path."

On the way to a dream, there were times I did not recognize myself.

Yet, I found the grace to whisper, "Thank you for peeling away the layers."

On the way to a dream, there were times I was so beaten and so battered.

Yet, I found the strength to whisper, "Thank you for making me stronger."

On the way to a dream, there were times I made grand mistakes.

Yet, I found the wisdom to whisper, "Thank you for the lessons learned."

On the way to a dream, there were times I simply failed.

Yet, I found the humility to whisper, "Thank you for the chance to try once more."

On the way to a dream, there were times I believed I could no longer continue.

Yet, I found the faith to whisper, "Thank you for but one more step."

On the way to a dream, there were times I knew of heartbreak.

Yet, I found the place in my heart to whisper, "Thank you for the chance to love you."

This is the moral of the story: express gratitude.

June 17

*When your footsteps and thoughts carry you down the same
path your heart and soul are directing you, you will know without
a doubt that you are headed in the right direction.*
—Molly Friedenfeld

When you trust your path.

When you find inner peace.

When you know your truth.

When you walk with faith.

When you come to know joy.

When you express gratitude.

When you no longer fear.

When you learn the lessons.

When you fully shine your light.

When you achieve a dream.

When you embrace who you are.

When you love the life you are living.

It will show.

June 18

I would like to learn, or remember, how to live.
—Annie Dillard

Remember what brought you to this place.
Patience. Discipline. Perseverance. Faith.
These shall see you through.

Remember what you have become.
Humble. Strong. Courageous. Capable.
These shall define your journey.

Remember what you believe in.
Hope. Dreams. Light. Love.
These shall carry your burdens.

Remember what you have learned.
Trust more. Worry less. Trust more.
These shall calm your heart.

Remember what it is you seek.
Truth. Joy. Peace. Home.
These shall be all you find.

Remember.

June 19

What catches your attention can change day to day.
But what catches your attention day after day is what you should pay attention to.
—Khang Kijarro Nguyen

The universe offers its signs.

Signs that say, "No fear."

The universe offers its signs.

Signs that say, "Thank you."

The universe offers its signs.

Signs that say, "Life is good."

The universe offers its signs.

Signs that say, "This is the way."

The universe offers its signs.

Signs that say, "Stay the course."

The universe offers its signs.

Signs that say, "Welcome home."

The universe offers its signs.

You must make sure you are paying attention.

June 20

When you believe in someone you profoundly increase their ability to have faith in themselves and achieve. When you love someone you imprint on their heart something so powerful that it changes the trajectory of their life. When you do both, you set into motion, a gift to the world...because those who are believed in and loved understand the beauty of a legacy and the absolute duty of paying it forward.
—Jason Versey

Dear Friend,

You do not have to suffer in silence.
Someone is hoping to listen.
So you won't have to suffer.

You do not have to be okay.
Someone is there for you.
So you will be okay.

You do not have to cling so tightly.
Someone is waiting to catch you.
So you can simply let go.

You do not have to know the way.
Someone is offering a light.
So you may find your way.

You do not have to worry.
Someone is believing in you.
So you can finally trust.

You do not have to always stand tall.
Someone is hitting their knees.
So you may be lifted up.

Love,

Someone

June 21

Having once been afraid of the darkness, I shall now not fear my light.

Having once been afraid of the loneliness, I shall now not fear my own company.

Having once been afraid of the fall, I shall now not fear my ability to soar.

Having once been afraid of the questions, I shall now not fear my answers.

Having once been afraid of the nightmares, I shall now not fear my dreams.

Having once been afraid of the lies, I shall now not fear my truth.

Having once been afraid of the brokenness, I shall now not fear my pieces coming together.

Having once been afraid of the silence, I shall now not fear my heart's whisper.

Having once been afraid, I shall now not fear.

June 22

If you want to find the trail, if you want to find yourself, you must explore your dreams alone. You must grow at a slow pace in a dark cocoon of loneliness so you can fly like wind, like wings, when you awaken.
—Francesca Lia Block

This is a story.

I find myself somewhere between want and need.

Somewhere between that I desire and all I cannot live without.

I find myself somewhere between the easy path and the difficult road.

Somewhere between my comfort zone and where I must travel.

I find myself somewhere between hope and faith.

Somewhere between feeling the dream can happen and believing the dream is destined to come true.

I find myself somewhere between doubt and trust.

Somewhere between being filled with questions and knowing the answers.

I find myself somewhere between fear and courage.

Somewhere between being afraid to take action and doing what must be done despite the fear.

I find myself somewhere between brokenness and completeness.

Somewhere between searching for the missing pieces and recognizing I am already whole.

This is the moral of the story: I may not yet be where I want to be. But for finding myself, I know the direction I must go.

June 23

Time changes everything except something within
us which is always surprised by change.
—Thomas Hardy

Time has changed me.

Much has been worn away.

The jagged edges now smooth.

The mistakes of the past now lessons learned.

The brokenness now devoid of pain.

Time has healed me.

Much has been erased.

The jagged scars are now barely visible.

The mistakes of the past are now memories fading.

The brokenness is now no longer indelible.

Time has moved me.

Much has been found.

The jagged road is now leading me home.

The mistakes of the past are now markers pointing me forward.

The brokenness is now a sign of my strength.

Time has discovered me.

Much has been misunderstood.

The jagged pieces of me simply needed time to be put together.

The mistakes of the past were never meant to define me.

The brokenness within me only served to make me whole.

June 24

A test lies always ahead of you.
—*Freedom Goodbird*

This is another life chat.

Life: A test awaits you.
Me: I know, it draws near.

Life: Are you ready?
Me: How am I to know?

Life: Tell me the lesson you have learned.
Me: I can handle, come what may.

Life: Tell me the fear you have overcome.
Me: The fear of failing.

Life: Tell me the whisper you hear.
Me: I am capable and strong.

Life: Tell me the truth you know.
Me: I will not be broken.

Life: Tell me the outcome you seek.
Me: To have grown from this test.

Life: Tell me the guides you shall use.
Me: Trust and faith.

Life: Tell me the key to succeeding.
Me: Do not ever quit.

Me: Tell me, am I ready?
Life: You are ready.

June 25

Who you are is too vast to be captured by the reflection of a mirror, classified by the state of your attitude, or categorized by the opinions of others. Therefore, if any of these are defining you, you have yet to be defined.
—Craig D. Lounsbrough

I view myself through a different lens.

I do not see myself as an inspiration.

I simply have made the choice to live an inspired life.

I do not see myself as amazing.

I simply have made the choice to occasionally amaze myself.

I do not see myself as special.

I simply have made the choice to accept my uniqueness.

I do not see myself as gifted or talented.

I simply have made the choice to offer the very best I have.

I do not see myself as others see me.

I simply have made the choice to try and reflect the light I see in them.

I view myself through a different lens.

June 26

This is a story.

For a child. For your child. For the child in you.

My life. As a broken crayon.

Blue
I felt broken. For I knew sadness. And it seemed to touch all the parts of my world. But I peeled back my wrapper and colored a most-brilliant sky. Reminding myself to always look up, for sadness comes for looking down.

Yellow
I felt broken. For I knew fear. And it was a fear of the dark and all things I did not know. But I peeled back my wrapper and colored a most-brilliant sun. Reminding myself that light will always remove the darkness, and I need not be afraid.

Green
I felt broken. For I knew envy. And it was for comparing myself to others. But I peeled back my wrapper and colored a most-brilliant field of grasses. Reminding myself, like each blade of grass, my blessings are so many. And as I count my blessings, I have no time for comparison.

Red
I felt broken. For I knew anger. And it was for all the hurts and wrongs done me. But I peeled back my wrapper and colored a most-brilliant heart. Reminding myself that with every beat of my heart, I am able to forgive, heal, and love again.

White

I felt broken. For I knew invisibility. And it was for believing no one knew of my hopes. But I peeled back my wrapper and colored a brilliant list of dreams that no one could see. Reminding myself that my hopes and dreams have been written, even if no one else ever knows.

This is the moral of the story: If you are feeling broken, peel back your wrapper to reveal your true colors. Use that to color your brilliance.

June 27

I heard a voice that told me I'm essential. How all my fears are limiting my potential.
Said it's time to step into the light and use every bit of power I have inside.
—India Arie

I heard a voice that told me, "You are essential."

You mean I'm important? I'm absolutely necessary?

And I wondered, who might speak such things of me?

I heard a voice that told me, "All your fears are limiting your potential."

You mean I'm capable of more? You believe in me?

And I wondered, who might speak such things of me?

I heard a voice that told me, "It's time to step into the light."

You mean you want to see me and all my imperfections? You do not fear my scars?

And I wondered, who might speak such things of me?

I heard a voice that told me, "It's time to use every bit of power inside of you."

You mean I am strong enough? I can do this?

And I wondered, who might speak such things of me?

I heard a voice.

And I finally realized, it was the very voice of self-love.

June 28

Sometimes our stop-doing list needs to be bigger than our to-do list.
—Patti Digh

Your list of "things to do" may not be exactly what you may think.

I'd like to share my list, in hopes it might help you, as you prepare to face the challenge set before you.

1. Untangle
2. Unpack
3. Unzip
4. Unfold
5. Understand

Untangle. Untangle the past. Understand that as you remain wrapped up in what once was, the used-to-be, that which you cannot change, you are prevented from moving forward.

Unpack. Unpack your fears. Lay them out and take a real good look at them. Ask yourself difficult questions about them. Where were they created? Why do they still take up so much space in your life?

Unzip. Unzip your doubts and excuses. Expose them. Watch as they shrink in the light. You see, they prefer to exist in the darkness. That is where they breathe and grow. That is when they come to life.

Unfold. Unfold your wings. Unfold yourself. So many times, you have played it safe, played small, downplayed your gifts, allowed yourself to be contained. For the past. For your fears. For your excuses. It is time to stop playing small. Unfold yourself.

Understand. Understand, in the end, life is not a checklist. It was never intended to be a list we check off, so we can move on to the next thing. Learn to enjoy the process of unfolding. Allow yourself to be present in the moment. Do not be in such a hurry for what comes next. What is now matters most.

June 29

Those who are truly grateful are deeply moved by the privilege of living.
—Auliq-Ice

It was a gift I offered. My smile.
You repaid me with the beauty of yours.

It was a gift I offered. My hand.
You repaid me by allowing me to help you stand.

It was a gift I offered. My words.
You repaid me by simply listening to the whispers.

It was a gift I offered. My friendship.
You repaid me for letting me walk this path with you.

It was a gift I offered. My love.
You repaid me by showing me my love was valued.

It was a gift I offered.
And yet, I am indebted to you.

June 30

You can find me somewhere in between inspiring others, working on myself, staying positive, and chasing my dreams.
—Anonymous

I am not lost, I am simply heading somewhere I've never been.

I am not wandering aimlessly, I am simply following a path to somewhere only I can know.

I am not fearful of the darkness, I am simply choosing somewhere the light always shines.

I am not hard to find, I am simply somewhere I was not standing yesterday.

I am not defined by the voices of "cannot," I am simply going somewhere they whisper my truth.

I am not deterred by the impossible, I am simply trusting there is somewhere dreams come true.

Should you come looking for me, this is where you will find me.

And should you go looking for yourself, I hope you find yourself there as well.

July 1

The cave you fear to enter holds the treasure you seek.
—Joseph Campbell

It seems that too often, we come to fear the finish.

Worrying about how difficult the journey might be or what it might require of us to get there.

And for sitting in the fear, some never start, and many never finish.

To this I simply say, "Fear not the finish."

Fear not the finish.
Fear never starting.

Fear not the struggle to finish.
Fear forgetting to enjoy the journey.

Fear not the distant finish.
Fear quitting before you find it.

Fear not being last to the finish.
Fear finishing alone.

Fear not the difficult finish.
Fear choosing the easy path.

Fear not the unseen finish.
Fear trusting only what you can see.

Fear not the finish.
Fear not living before you arrive there.

Fear not the finish.

July 2

*That's the thing about lessons, you always learn them
when you don't expect them or want them.*
—Cecelia Ahern

These are seven life lessons to learn.

1. Life does not deal everyone a fair hand.

It is up to each of us to get the most out of the cards we've been given.

2. Life is sometimes difficult.

It is not meant to bring about failure, but to teach us how to succeed.

3. Life is not interested in your cannot, your excuses, or your limits.

It wants to know what you can, what results you want, and what your possibilities are.

4. Life will take every opportunity it can to kick you when you are down.

It is trying to tell you, "That is not where you belong." So get up.

5. Life often hides its greatest gifts amongst the thorns.

It is the warrior willing to dip into the pain, who finds the prize.

6. Life will place many burdens before you.

It is for you to decide which are meant to strengthen and which serve only to drag you down. Know which to pick up.

7. Life repeatedly asks, "Have you done the work?"

And then, it sets forth its challenge to find out your answer.

July 3

Success is most often achieved by those who don't know that failure is inevitable.
—Coco Chanel

When I consider how success is achieved, I have come to the conclusion it revolves around four basic principles.

Belief

You must have an unwavering belief that success can and will be achieved. Trusting you have the ability, skill, grit, and potential to reach the goals you set for yourself.

That is not to say there will never be questions or doubts or even setbacks. But these cannot override the faith you place in yourself. And they should never keep you from chasing a dream that seems well beyond where you now stand.

Intention

You must be purpose-driven. Goal-focused. And the intent should be to raise your own bar. To improve upon your practices, skill set, frame of mind, and knowledge.

That is not to say that everything you do must require intensity and focus and commitment. But you cannot afford to allow complacency to replace your intentions. Nor can you let excuses fill the space where your dreams should reside.

Consistency

You must, with consistency, move toward your goals. The steps you take must become regular, habitual, at the center of your decision making. The goal or dream becomes not only what you do, but begins to define who you are.

This is not to say it must become all encompassing, all consuming. Balance remains a key to anything healthy. But excellence is established over time, and through consistent attention to improving.

Insistency

You must insist upon the structures and practices and guidelines you set for yourself. You must, with diligence and fidelity, do the work set before you. And then, demand excellence from and for yourself.

This is not to say the plan doesn't change or you will not encounter failures along the way. But you do not give up when those things happen. You learn, you grow, you make adjustments to the practices and even the course you are on. But you do not quit.

Belief. Intention. Consistency. Insistency. The keys to success. None of which are beyond any of us.

July 4

Defeat is not the worst of failures. Not to have tried is the true failure.
—George E. Woodberry

It may look like defeat.

But please know, my victories cannot often be seen. For they are found in the smallest of decisions. To simply try again. To simply rise to my feet. To simply believe I can do this once more.

My victories rarely able to be measured by human instruments. Times I've danced with my angels. Moments I've jumped despite not seeing the net. Instances of knowing goose bumps and breathlessness. Battles I've won over demons and fears others cannot imagine.

These are my personal victories. Seen by few, understood by few, celebrated by few. For they come without fanfare. Without arms raised high. Without much more than a whispered, "You can do this."

And should I stumble and fall short of the finish line, it does not mean I have been defeated. For in daring to bring myself to the start of the journey, I knew a victory.

And should I never attain the dreams I dream, it does not mean I have been defeated. For in daring to dream the impossible, I knew a victory.

It may look like defeat.

Do not be fooled. Today, I shall celebrate a victory. For I made the decision to try once more.

July 5

In the end, though, maybe we must all give up trying to pay back the people in this world who sustain our lives. In the end, maybe it's wiser to surrender before the miraculous scope of human generosity and to just keep saying thank you, forever and sincerely, for as long as we have voices.
—Elizabeth Gilbert

I thought of you, and it brought a smile.

For your strength inspired me to try again.

I thought you, and it brought a smile.

For your courage helped me take another step.

I thought of you, and it brought a smile.

For your faith filled me with hope.

I thought of you, and it brought a smile.

For your dreams made me believe in mine.

I thought of you, and it brought a smile.

For your kindness changed me for the better.

I thought of you, and it brought a smile.

For your prayers lifted me from my knees.

I thought of you, and it brought a smile.

For your friendship told me I am not alone.

I thought of you, and it brought a smile.

For you, I am so very grateful.

July 6

Without Your Opponent, You are no Victor.
—Anajo Black

The opponent—a story.

I sent coach a text last night, asking if it was too late to stop in for a workout. The body was tired. The day was long. The hour was getting late. I was almost hoping he would say call it a night.

Excuses vs. results

He responded that he was getting ready to do an "evil little ditty" himself. But, as he put it, a "recovery type workout," and he had drawn up something similar for me, so come on in. I was almost hoping the plan was going to be easy.

Motivation vs. discipline

Not sure why I passed over the "evil little ditty" in his message and focused on the "recovery" part of the message. At this point, I should have known better. The work was difficult. The rep count was high. The "quit" was present. I was almost hoping there was a time cap.

Comfort zone vs. growth

There seemed no end to the reps. Sprints and burpees and sit-ups and double-unders and Airdyne calories. With each flip of another card, a feeling of resignation. The pile didn't seem to be getting any smaller. And the clock just kept on ticking. I was almost hoping coach would say, "Shut it down."

Give up vs. finish

The "recovery" workout ended 56:16 later. No crowd to cheer for me. No medal hung round my neck. No PR to smile about. Simply another workout completed. I was almost hoping I could have finished it in better time.

Me vs. me

This is the moral of the story: There is always an opponent. And you always get to decide which one wins.

July 7

In a gentle way, you can shake the world.
—Mahatma Gandhi

For a child. For your child. For the child in you.

Dear Child,

In a world slipping into darkness, a light is needed. Shine yours. Be it with a smile, a kind word, or an act of love. Shine it for the entire world to see.

In a world hoping to silence the honest, a truth is needed. Speak yours. Be it in a whisper, shouted from the mountaintop, or through an act of love. Speak it for the entire world to hear.

In a world filling itself with violence, a peace is needed. Teach yours. Be it with forgiveness, a humble apology, or an act of love. Teach it for the entire world to know.

In a world bent on finding ugliness, a beauty is needed. Share yours. Be it with a song, a poem, or an act of love. Share it for the entire world to feel.

For you see my child, your light and truth and peace and beauty may not change the entire world, but it will change mine.

Love,

Me

July 8

Just remember to say THANK YOU sometimes, for
all of these everyday extraordinary gifts.
—Scott Stabile

The gifts.

You gave to me the gift of your time.

And I can never repay you for the precious moments.

You gave to me the gift of your smiles.

And I can never repay you for all the smiles I will have, for remembering the laughter we shared.

You gave to me the gift of your dreams.

And I can never repay you for sharing these priceless pieces of yourself with me.

You gave to me the gift of your friendship.

And I can never repay you for that which a value cannot be placed upon.

You gave to me the gift of your trust.

And I can never repay you, but only hope to always honor it.

You gave to me your gifts. And I can only offer my heartfelt "Thank you."

And your only response need be: "You are welcome."

July 9

Someone out there is looking for exactly what you've got...and will never try and undercut your value or question your worth. Some things in life just can't be bartered over or placed on the sale rack—and your self-worth is at the top of the list.
—Mandy Hale

Your worth.

For a child. For your child. For the child in you.

Dear Child,

Your worth is not tied to how many friends or followers you have.

Your worth is found in how you treat the friends and strangers who pass through your every day.

Your worth is not tied to how you portray yourself through social media.

Your worth is found in how you live your life when no one else is looking at you.

Your worth is not tied to any number, be it weight or height or grade-point average or zip code or likes.

Your worth is found in making kindness and caring your number-one priority.

Your worth is not tied to making a team, belonging to a club, conforming to the crowd.

Your worth is found in doing your best, welcoming others in, being true to the values instilled in you.

Your worth is not tied to what others may say about you.

Your worth is found in the words you speak to yourself.

Your worth is not tied to the times you stumble or fall or fail.

Your worth is found in your willingness to keep showing up and to keep trying.

Your worth is not tied to a price tag.

Your worth is found in coming to understand that the gifts you have to offer are priceless.

Love,

Me

July 10

Have you ever had a dream so strong it slapped you
in the face every time you looked away?
—Joyce Rachelle

A dream was given you.

Perhaps not for safekeeping or to harbor it, but so you may chase it. And it longs to be pursued. Are you willing?

A dream was given you.

Perhaps so grand and impossible it frightens you. But those are simply illusions. And it only requires faith to attain. Are you hope-filled?

A dream was given you.

Perhaps so distant and far away it seems beyond your grasp. But time and space have no relevance in matters of the heart. And it is closer than you know. Are you reaching?

A dream was given you.

Perhaps you have not come to realize what it is yet. But the universe knows. And it speaks in whispers of it. Are you listening?

A dream was given you.

Perhaps it simply sits waiting, but wanting to know your truth. And its only question shall be: "Are you a dreamer?"

July 11

My burdens. They buckled me.
More than once.

My fears. They paralyzed me.
More than once.

My weaknesses. They limited me.
More than once.

My demons. They defeated me.
More than once.

My excuses. They defined me.
More than once.

My failures. They broke me.
More than once.

My burdens, fears, weaknesses, demons, excuses, failures.

More than once, I have risen above them.

I will again today. Once more.

July 12

*I like cancelled plans. And empty bookstores. I like rainy days and
thunderstorms. And quiet coffee shops. I like messy beds and over-worn
pajamas. Most of all, I like the small joys that a simple life brings.*
—Unknown

This is a story.

Been taking time to sit and think
To slowly sip my drink

Been taking time to just unwind
Trying to clear my mind

Been taking time to travel the road
For a chance to lessen the load

Been taking time to in the great outdoors
Sitting by a fire and making s'mores

Been taking time to quiet the noise
Remembering the simply joys

Been taking time to again exhale
Letting the wind refill my sail

Been taking time for long-lost walks
And those little heart-to-heart talks

Been taking time for clearing space
Putting a smile upon my face

Been taking time to simply unplug
Giving the heartstrings a gentle tug

Been taking time to simply be
Rediscovering all that is me

This is the moral of the story: Life is not simply about the time you've been given. It's about the time you take.

July 13

Once you say "I can't," you suppress the left over passion in you. But when you say "I can," you spark your inner power to make it happen. You can!
—Israelmore Ayivor

It has been awhile since Life and I had time to talk. So we took a little break and did a little talking.

This is another life chat.

Me: There are times you can seem like more than I am able to handle.
Life: Yes, I can.

Me: There are times you can seem like you are trying to break me.
Life: Yes, I can.

Me: There are times you can seem like you are bigger than my abilities.
Life: Yes, I can.

Me: There are times you can seem like you are out to get me.
Life: Yes, I can.

Me: There are times you can seem like you are bent on confusing me.
Life: Yes, I can.

Me: You are not really offering much help.
Life: I am simply agreeing with your observations. Did you want more?

Me: Yes. How am I to respond when you are like that? When you show up to question my ability, my strength, my faith?
Life: My dear child, you already know how to respond. You simply say, "Yes, I can."

July 14

I know none of this seems very believable. It probably doesn't even make sense. But for once in your life, please, I am asking you to trust me. Trust yourself.
—Charles Yu

This is a story.

Once again, you faced the day. And all it held.

There is strength and courage in that simple act.

Once again, you took steps forward. Despite the obstacles.

There is faith and trust in that simple act.

Once again, you stood tall. Refusing to bow.

There is growth and power in that simple act.

Once again, you chose to believe in you. A priceless gift.

There is hope and love in that simple act.

This is the moral of the story: Strength and courage. Faith and trust. Growth and power. Hope and love. All found in the simple act of being you.

July 15

The difference between a successful person and others is not a lack
of strength, not a lack of knowledge, but rather a lack in will.
—*Vince Lombardi Jr.*

This is your pep talk.

You don't have to lace 'em up.

You don't have to log those miles.

You don't have to make it to the gym.

You don't have to take that spin, yoga, HIIT, or Zumba class.

You don't have hit the track after work.

You don't have to do one more rep, set, or mile.

You don't have to challenge yourself.

You don't have to face your fears or move beyond your comfort zone.

You don't have to climb that mountain yet again today.

You don't have to. But you will.

It is what you do.

It has become a part of who you are.

A piece of the fabric that now defines who you want to be and what you want to accomplish.

You don't have to. But you will.

Discipline. Perseverance. Strength. Faith.

You don't have to. But you will.

You've just been pep-talked.

July 16

Shine your light and make a positive impact on the world; there is nothing so honorable as helping improve the lives of others.
—Roy T. Bennett

Your light inspired me.

I saw you shine, and I gave myself permission to do the same.

Your courage inspired me.

I saw you face your fear, and I was compelled to do the same.

Your strength inspired me.

I saw you rise once again, and I knew I must do the same.

Your faith inspired me.

I saw you go forward not knowing the outcome, and I believed I could do the same.

Your kindness inspired me.

I saw you reach out to another, and I understood my purpose is to do the same.

Your discipline inspired me.

I saw you cast aside your excuses, and I realized I was able to do the same.

You inspired me. And I will never be the same.

July 17

Each step you take reveals a new horizon. You have taken the
first step today. Now, I challenge you to take another.
—Dan Poynter

You do not need to climb the entire mountain today.

You simply need to take the very next step.

You do not need to know the entire path today.

You simply need to know the very next step

You do not need to travel the entire distance today.

You simply need to be willing to walk the very next step.

You do not need to see the entire road stretched out before you.

You simply need to trust the very next step.

You do not need to worry about the entire journey.

You simply need to believe in the very next step.

One step. Then one step more. That is how the mountain is always climbed.

July 18

When you have nothing to offer, love gives abundantly.
—E'yen A. Gardner

Dear Friend,

I know not of your internal struggle. The battles you must silently wage. For words often fail in matters of brokenness.

But I know of your heart's ache. And I send to you the love I hold in my heart.

I know not of your constant strength. The effort you must invest simply to rise each day. For burdens weighing you down are not visible to the eye.

But I know of your heart's heaviness. And I send to you the love I hold in my heart.

I know not of your emptiness. The void you must now fill. For the space between what once was and what now is cannot be measured.

But I know of your heart's loneliness. And I send to you the love I hold in my heart.

So much I do not know, my friend. But I want you to know, you are held in my heart.

And I send to you my love. In hopes it makes a difference.

Love,

Me

July 19

If you want to conquer the anxiety of life, live in the moment, live in the breath.
—Amit Ray

I have much work left to do. But I do not fear where I stand this day. Nor do I worry about what must be done between now and then.

For all I can control is what I do in the present. And thus, it gets and keeps my attention, my time, and is my priority.

And by remaining in the present, discipline—and discipline alone—is what leads me through the challenge set before me.

When I move outside of the present, looking back at what I did not do or looking ahead to what needs to be done, I allow worry and stress and doubt and motivation and fear and excuses to become characters in my story.

And they begin to take on a life of their own. Speaking lines that grow ever louder. Consuming pages in my book that take away from the script I am actually wanting to pen.

So while my dream sits waiting in the distance, I am content to build the steps toward it one decision, one run, one day at a time.

Trusting, that in this present moment, discipline will place another stepping stone on my path. And my dream will move ever closer.

July 20

When all the water has gone, only the largest stones remain in the riverbed.
—African proverb

This is a story about a rock in the river.

Years ago, I worked in a residential setting for abused and addicted youth. As a counselor, my role was to help these teenagers make it to graduation, and ultimately, to emancipation from the home.

One particular young man had a long way to go and a hard road to travel to get to that point. The level of abuse he had suffered, I could not imagine. His level of addiction belied his young life.

After months of intensive work with him, I was feeling as if we were making progress. But I showed up for work only to find out he had run away from the home. As few days later, he was picked up, wasted. He was sent to detox, and ultimately he made his way back into the criminal-justice system.

I felt as if I had failed him. The hours, the time, the work invested, all seemed for naught.

And yet, here is what my mentor said to me: "You have to realize, you were his rock in the river. He was going along, and then he came upon you. He had to change directions because of you."

"But, we failed," I said.

She simply replied, "No. His life, his path, is forever changed because you were a rock in the river. He can never go back to the path he was traveling."

It would be years later that my path and his would cross again. He remembered me. And I remembered him.

We spoke only a few words of the past. He, no longer the young man I thought I had failed. Me, now immersed in my career as an educator.

What brought us together, you might ask? He wanted to proudly introduce his daughter to me. She was a student at my school. And oh, how he beamed.

I would never see him again. But, as I recall that meeting, I sensed he was going to be okay.

This is the moral of the story: Most times, we never get to know where our influence ends or how we impact another. And so, I have tried to live a life being "a rock in the river."

Knowing, as others pass by, I am forever changing their course. Therefore, may I always strive to offer a kind word, a safe place to land, a guiding light, a gentle and loving heart. Tomorrow, we all have a chance to be a "rock in the river." How will we choose to alter another's course?

July 21

Accept yourself, your strengths, your weaknesses, your truths,
and know what tools you have to fulfill your purpose.
—Steve Maraboli

When strength is needed,

Call upon your history.

For within your story, are chapters dedicated to how strong you have always been.

When hope is needed,

Call upon your prayers.

For within your silent whispers, are found all you believe in.

When faith is needed,

Call upon your dreams.

For within your ability to imagine the impossible, is a true leap of faith.

When bravery is needed,

Call upon your heart.

For within your willingness to love again is the greatest act of courage.

Your history. Your prayers. Your dreams. Your heart. Call upon them.

They hold all that is needed.

July 22

Don't sell yourself short. You may never have proof of your importance, but you are more important than you think.
—Robert Fulghum

When you measure your strength, do not forget the times you simply and quietly stood tall.

For there is power in finding your place to stand.

When you measure your courage, do not forget the times you simply could not stop the trembling.

For there is bravery in knowing you are afraid, yet still walking into the darkness.

When you measure your success, do not forget the times you have fallen short.

For there is triumph in overcoming the desire to surrender.

When you measure your ability, do not forget the times you said, "I can't."

For there is a history of you constantly proving yourself wrong.

When you measure you, do not discount your strength, courage, success, or ability.

For there is nothing gained in selling yourself short.

July 23

A dreamer, I walked enchanted, and nothing held me back.
—Daphne du Maurier

I am a dreamer.

I always have been.

The process is really quite simple.

First, you have to dream.

And it should be of that beyond what you can perhaps even comprehend.

Next, you have to believe.

And it should be not that the dream will come true, but that within you, exists the ability to make it so.

Then, you have to listen to the dream.

And it should be a voice that constantly and quietly whispers, even above the fears and questions and doubts and excuses calling your name.

Finally, you have to be willing.

And it should be a willingness that requires the best parts of you, requires mistakes and setbacks and hard work, requires you to finally and completely invest in yourself.

Dream, my friend, dream.

July 24

I have a habit of letting my imagination run away from me. It always comes back though...drenched with possibilities.
—Valaida Fullwood

I do not know where my motivation wanes.

But I imagine I would not allow my discipline to be concerned with it.

I do not know where my comfort zone is.

But I imagine I would not truly take refuge there.

I do not know where my limit is.

But I imagine I would not accept being confined by it.

I do not know where my courage ends.

But I imagine I would not stop at that point.

I do not know where my dreams become impossible.

But I imagine I would not believe that as a reality.

Imagine.

July 25

There is nothing more powerful than a humble person with
a warrior spirit who is driven by a bigger purpose.
—Jeff Osterman

There is power in speaking softly.

There is power in remaining humble.

There is power in quietly getting it done.

There is power in a gentle spirit.

There is power in being a peaceful warrior

There is power in acting with kindness.

There is power in finding your purpose.

There is power in getting outside yourself.

There is power in lifting another.

There is a power in you.

May you know it and always use it for good.

July 26

The strongest of all warriors are these two—Time and Patience.
—Leo Tolstoy

There are times I am guilty of lacking patience.

For wishing I were further along my journey.

Not realizing, I am not yet prepared for what awaits me down the road.

There are times I am guilty of lacking patience.

For wishing I did not have to deal with what is set before me.

Not realizing I must first pass this test before taking on another.

There are times I am guilty of lacking patience.

For wishing I already possessed the skills and tools I shall need.

Not realizing these are crafted over time.

There are times I am guilty of lacking patience.

For wishing I were strong enough to not feel broken.

Not realizing, amongst the brokenness, I found true strength.

There are times I simply need to be patient.

July 27

Roll all your windows down. Crank up the music. Let someone else make the bed. You deserve that. You deserve the beautiful life you have made. You, deserve EVERYTHING.
—This Is Us

The words above are not my words. They're taken from a fictitious television show.

Perhaps you watched it. Perhaps you even shed a tear, or two.

And as I listened to these words, I could not help but think of you.

And I wondered, did you ever consider these words were being spoken directly to you?

For how many times have you worked from a model of deficit, convincing yourself you do not deserve all the things your heart holds closest?

Whether it be happiness; fulfillment; peace; to simply believe in a dream, an unwavering love.

Whatever it is, you must realize, you are worthy and deserving. You always have been. Always.

You must first believe. And then, you must act accordingly.

Roll all the windows down, crank up the music. Sing your song. Dance your dance.

Smile at life. Chase those dreams. Live and love with a heart wide open.

And if I could, but for a moment, place your face between my hands, I would look you in the eyes and softly whisper, "You deserve everything."

July 28

I love watching what you become when life thinks it has you cornered.
—Curtis Tyrone Jones

The road set before you, it must be traveled.

Not for what waits at the end of the journey.

But for what you find along the way.

The challenge set before you, it must be faced.

Not for what waits after it has been endured.

But for how you choose to respond when it becomes difficult.

The fear set before you, it must be overcome.

Not for what waits after your courage is on display.

But for how you learn to stop the trembling.

The brokenness set before you, it must be embraced.

Not for what waits after you feel whole again.

But for what you gain as you pick up the pieces.

The mountain set before you, it must be climbed.

Not for what waits on the other side.

But for who you become during the ascent.

July 29

This is my wish for you: Comfort on difficult days, smiles when sadness intrudes, rainbows to follow the clouds, laughter to kiss your lips, sunsets to warm your heart, hugs when spirits sag, beauty for your eyes to see, friendships to brighten your being, faith so that you can believe, confidence for when you doubt, courage to know yourself, patience to accept the truth, Love to complete your life.
—Ralph Waldo Emerson

This is my wish, for you.

Dear Friend,

I wish for you goose bumps and Mufasas.
Fairy-tale endings and dreams coming true.

I wish for you less of what hurts you and more of what brings you joy.
Less worry. More peace. Less doubt. More trust.

I wish for you finish lines and amazing times.
Races run and adventures known.

I wish for you magic and unicorns.
The heart of a child. The hope of a dreamer.

I wish for you joy unfolding and simple blessings too many to count.
Mornings on the deck. Nights chasing fireflies.

I wish for you emptiness and fulfillment.
A heart empty of pain. A life filled with happiness.

I wish for you better.
Better than you have ever known. Better than merely pieces.

I wish for you love unwavering and unending.
For the moment. For all of time.

I wish for you.
This day. And always.

Love,

Me

July 30

The meaning of life is to make life be more.
—Will Advise

I wish for you more than "I'm fine."

I wish for you more than "I'm okay."

I wish for you more than "I can't."

I wish for you more than "What if…"

I wish for you more than "I'm afraid."

I wish for you more than "Why me?"

I wish for you more than "I failed."

I wish for you more than "I give up."

I wish for you more than "I'm not good enough."

I wish for you more than "This is impossible."

I wish for you. More.

July 31

In walking, we acquire more of less.
—Robert Moor

I wish for you less anxiousness.

I wlsh for you less fear and doubt.

I wish for you less excuses.

I wish for you less settling.

I wish for you less brokenness.

I wish for you less clinging to used-to-be.

I wish for you less looking back.

I wish for you less troubled waters.

I wish for you less ache in your heart.

I wish for you. Less.

And yet, I wish for you more.

August 1

We don't have to be fast; we simply have to be steady and move in the right direction. Direction is always going to trump speed.
—Unknown

Achieving a dream:

1. Deciding upon a direction

2. Steadiness of resolve

3. The art of patience

4. Commitment greater than excuses

5. Discipline over motivation

6. Learning from failure

7. Willingness to change

8. Acceptance of the struggles

9. Constant forward movement

10. Staying true to the direction

11. Remaining humble

12. Unwavering belief

August 2

On the other side of your maximum fear, are all of the best things in life.
—Will Smith

This is a story.

In my life, I have known powerful fear.

I was afraid to stand up for what I truly deserved.

And so there was no chance I would ever receive it.

I was afraid to take the path with no light.

And so there was no chance I would see what waited beyond the darkness.

I was afraid to move beyond my comfort zone.

And so there was no chance I would be free of my limits.

I was afraid to take myself to the ledge.

And so there was no chance I would ever feel my wings.

I was afraid to show my imperfections and scars.

And so there was no chance I would be seen as beautiful.

I was afraid of opening myself to the hurt again.

And so there was no chance I would feel anything.

I was afraid to say, "I love you."

And so there was no chance I would hear it echoed.

I was afraid to chase after my craziest dream.

And so there was no chance it would ever come true.

This is the moral of the story: the true power of fear is not what it keeps you from doing, but in what it steals from you—the chance to know.

August 3

Do not go where the path may lead, go instead
where there is no path and leave a trail.
—Ralph Waldo Emerson

I am blazing a new trail.
Unafraid where it may lead.

I am blazing a new trail.
A life beyond comfort.

I am blazing a new trail.
Embracing the ascent.

I am blazing a new trail.
Not fearing the descent.

I am blazing a new trail.
Earning scars along the way.

I am blazing a new trail.
Finding beauty within me.

I am blazing a new trail.
In my search for home.

I am blazing a new trail.
Where few dare wander.

I am blazing a new trail.
Ever yearning for growth.

I am blazing a new trail.
Toward an unwavering love.

Things to do: Become one with your trail.

August 4

The biggest adventure you can ever take is to live the life of your dreams.
—Oprah Winfrey

And so again today, I take off on another adventure.

Unknowns and challenges ahead of me.

And yet, I must venture forth.

Something whispers to me, "Chase the dream."

And so again today, I take off on another adventure.

Unknowns and challenges ahead of me.

And yet, I must venture forth.

Something whispers to me, "Something waits for you to arrive."

And so again today, I take off on another adventure.

Unknowns and challenges ahead of me.

And yet, I must venture forth.

Something whispers to me, "Do not be afraid; you will be okay."

And so again today, I take off on another adventure.

Unknowns and challenges ahead of me.

And yet, I must venture forth.

Something whispers to me, "Rise to the occasion."

And so again today, I take off on another adventure.

Unknowns and challenges ahead of me.

And yet, I must venture forth.

Something whispers to me, "You were created to do more than exist. You are meant to soar."

And so again today, I must venture forth.

August 5

We are all like poems. Some of us rhyme. Some don't. Some are Pulitzer prizes. Some
are just scribbles. And yet, we all possess a special kind of beauty that can either
heal or cut to the bone. One that can never quite be fathomed, nor forgotten.
—Sanober Khan

You will come to a place in your life that feels like an ending.
As if there is no more. As if, "now what."

You will come to a place in your life that feels like an ending.
As if there are no more words to write. As if a chapter has ended.

You will come to a place in your life that feels like an ending.
As if a door has finally closed. As if there are no more doors to open.

You will come to a place in your life that feels like an ending.
As if this is where you must remain. As if this is permanence.

You will come to a place in your life that feels like an ending.
As if the song has ended. As if the music is no more.

You will come to a place in your life that feels like an ending.
As if the dream has been lost. As if the dream has been realized.

You will come to a place in your life that feels like an ending.
But what you must always understand is that every ending is merely the chance for
a new beginning.

Things to do: Choose your "now what." Beautifully scribble on that blank page. Find
a window. Keep moving. Create your own music. Dream a new dream.

August 6

Your best teacher is the person offering you your greatest challenge.
—Cheryl Richardson

I am here to offer you an idea: "can't" and "impossible" and "failure" are perceptions and myths, not truths or facts.

I am here to offer you a dose of reality: your excuses will no longer hold you back when you finally decide to let go of them.

I am here to offer you some tough love: you brought yourself to this place, only you can extricate yourself from here.

I am here to offer you a secret: the secret to all things, be it happiness, success, peace, or love, is to choose that thing.

I am here to offer you a key: the key to opening the door before you, do not fear what's on the other side.

I am here to offer you a bit of hope: goodness and light and love have always triumphed. Always.

I am here to offer you pillars to a dream: patience, effort, perseverance, faith.

I am here to offer you the truth: you are amazing and strong and capable and worthy and beautiful.

Take what you need. Leave the rest.

August 7

There is much I have yet to learn.
Let me set myself to the lessons.

There is much I yet do not know.
Let me face the unknowns with faith.

There is much I have yet to envision.
Let me imagine the impossible.

There is much I have yet to try.
Let me ever show a willingness to dare.

There is much I have yet to accomplish.
Let me prepare to be successful.

There is much I have yet to master.
Let me never allow this to be my limit.

There is much I have yet to overcome.
Let me begin the ascent.

There is much. Let me embrace the power of yet.

August 8

Hope can be a powerful force. Maybe there's no actual magic in it,
but when you know what you hope for most and hold it like a light
within you, you can make things happen, almost like magic.
—Laini Taylor

This an open letter.

For my child. For your child. For the child in you.

Dear Child,

I hope you know a joy. A joy that is evident in your smile, in your words, in your daily prayers.

I hope you know a freedom. A freedom that allows you to spread your wings, allows you to wander where your heart leads, allows you to chase your rainbows.

I hope you know a strength. A strength that sees you through the difficult times, steadies you when you feel like falling, moves you forward when the road rises before you.

I hope you know a courage. A courage that grants you permission to dare greatly, to dream the impossible, to never be limited or contained by fear.

I hope you know a magic. A magic that helps you always to believe in dreams and fairy tales and unicorns.

I hope you know a love. A love that brings you joy. A love that sets you free. A love that gives you strength. A love that emboldens you. A love that simply feels like magic.

And most of all, I hope you dance.

Love,

Me

August 9

*When you have lost hope, you have lost everything. And when you
think all is lost, when all is dire and bleak, there is always hope.*
—Pittacus Lore

I hope you had a good day.
I hope you smiled and heard laughter.
I hope your high points were many.

I hope you knew moments of peace.
I hope you had your breath taken away.
I hope your tears were of joy.

I hope you chose to believe.
I hope you did not settle for your excuses.
I hope you leaned on your strength.

I hope you did more than survive.
I hope you thrived.
I hope you shined.

I hope you faced your fears.
I hope you trembled and still leapt.
I hope you danced.

I hope you fought again today.
I hope you fell forward.
I hope you celebrated you.

I hope you let go that you cannot control.
I hope you rejoiced in your blessings.
I hope you learned and grew.

I hope you lived life in full force.
I hope you loved yourself.
I hope you hoped.

I hope. For you.

August 10

I will only add, God bless you.
—Jane Austen

Dear Friend,

Tonight, my prayers shall be for you.

May sleep find you gently.

May peace of mind be your companion.

May worries not dwell in your heart.

May comfort settle over you.

May your pains and burdens fall away.

May you deeply rest.

May a quiet come to your mind.

May dreams carry you forward.

May you feel my love.

This, I pray for you.

August 11

For a child. For your child. For the child in you.

Some will watch simply to judge.
Let your actions allow for no deductions.

Some will watch simply to criticize.
Let your actions speak louder than their words.

Some will watch simply to cheer you on.
Let your actions silently express gratitude.

Some will watch simply to imitate.
Let your actions be worthy of this.

Some will watch simply to be inspired.
Let your actions move them to their own greatness.

Some will watch simply to find hope.
Let your actions provide them direction.

Some will watch simply to understand you.
Let your actions define your essence.

Some will watch simply to simply to learn.
Let your actions teach beautiful lessons.

Some will watch, but when no one does,
Let your actions remain the same.

August 12

Contentment comes from wanting what we need, not needing what we want.
—Wayne Gerard Trotman

This is a story.

I want to be stronger. Of mind. And body.
Yet gentle of word and heart.

I want to be more brave. Less fear. Less worry.
Yet still feel the trembling.

I want to be closer. To home. To the dream.
Yet always willing to wander.

I want to be more grounded. Connected. Rooted.
Yet ever willing to take flight.

I want to be steadier. Of faith. Of pace.
Yet able to endure having myself shaken.

I want to be more certain. Less doubt. Fewer questions.
Yet embracing of the unknown ahead.

I want to be better. In all phases of my life.
Yet grateful for who I have now become.

This is the moral of the story: Want what you may want. Yet never allow it to replace
what you truly need.

August 13

True discipline is really just self-remembering; no forcing or fighting is necessary.
—*Charles Eisenstein*

This is your pep talk.

You don't need to be motivated.
You have to be disciplined.

You don't need someone to say, "Get up."
You have dreams for that.

You don't need more time.
You have to prioritize your time.

You don't need to quit making excuses.
You have to stop using them.

You don't need to be held accountable.
You have to know what counts.

You don't need to rely on luck.
You have to lean on your faith.

You don't need to be told what to do.
You have to simply listen to your heart.

You don't need reasons to get it done.
You have the only reason you need: you.

You've just been pep-talked.

August 14

The chance to do it over again is called now.
—J. R. Rim

Today does not want to know of your old wounds.
It wants to know if you will do battle once more.

Today does not want to know of your past stories.
It wants to know if you will begin a new chapter.

Today does not want to know of your imagined fears.
It wants to know if you will face your currently reality.

Today does not want to know of your tiredness.
It wants to know if you will awaken to the dream.

Today does not want to know of your burdens.
It wants to know if you are strong enough to set them down.

Today does not want to know of your excuses.
It wants to know if you are finally going to rise above them.

Today does not want to know of your limits and walls.
It wants to know if you are ready to break free of them.

Today does not want to know of your failures.
It wants to know if you are willing to try again.

Today does not want to know of your heartache.
It wants to know if you are able to stitch yourself together.

Today does not want to know. It already knows.
That's why you were given another chance.

August 15

Today is your day to paint life in bold colors; set today's rhythm with your heart-drum; walk today's march with courage; create today as your celebration of life.
—Jonathan Lockwood Huie

Today, you will face your challenge with grace and grit.

Today, you will conquer your fear with trust and faith.

Today, you will move forward on your path with strength and patience.

Today, you will fulfill your promise with courage and conviction.

Today, you will shine your light with beauty and confidence.

Today, you will unfold your wings with belief and power.

Today, you will speak your truth with clarity and intention.

Today, you will count your blessings with joy and gratitude.

Today, you will grow into your self with love and acceptance.

Today. You will.

August 16

To fall down is to face the weakness of my humanity, test the mettle of my character, and push the limits of my strength. Therefore, falling down will tell me who I am far more clearly than most things I might learn when I'm standing up.
—Craig D. Lounsbrough

This is a story.

I have fallen. Many times. Tripped myself up.
Over things grand and small. I have gotten up. Every time.

I have fallen. Many times. Ever so hard.
Face first. I have gotten up. Every time.

I have fallen. Many times. Been broken.
Bear the scars. I have gotten up. Every time.

I have fallen. Many times. From great heights.
The plunge terrifying. I have gotten up. Every time.

I have picked up habits. Many times. Bad ones.
Costly ones. I have put them down. Every time.

I have picked up excuses. Many times. So many to carry.
They weigh heavy on me. I have put them down. Every time.

I have picked up fears. Many times. Some real.
Most imagined. I have put them down. Every time.

I have picked up burdens. Many times. Out of guilt.
Out of regret. I have put them down. Every time.

This is the moral of the story: You fall down. You get up. You pick it up. You put it down.
You get stronger. Every time.

August 17

You can't teach an old dog new tricks
—Proverb

This is a story.

Nearly three years ago, I joined my boy's gym. Before that, he had subtly hinted, on more than one occasion, that he would like to see me give CrossFit a try. I never shared with him why it took me so long to walk through those doors.

You see, truth is, I am a creature of habit. In many ways, a victim of my own routines and somewhat obsessive nature. And, although I like to think I am open to growth and change, I rely on what I know and what I do. Perhaps I am even set in my ways.

I was a runner. It's what I did. What I knew. I didn't lift things. I didn't jump on things. I simply ran. It was my comfort zone. My habit. My routine. So why change? Why try something new? I didn't see the need. What I was doing was working. Or so that's what I kept telling myself.

Truth is, it was more than that. Hard to put a name to it. It wasn't fear. It wasn't worry about embarrassing myself. It wasn't because I was too old. It wasn't because I might fail. But then again, maybe it was all of that.

I think my boy sensed all of this. For although he worked me harder than I had ever worked before, he kept me from some things. Maybe I wasn't ready. Maybe he was protecting me. Maybe he was afraid for me. Maybe he understood my routines. Slowly, he began adding skills and movements that produced repeated failure. Skills that would take months to learn. Skills that made me feel like a beginner, and thus they brought with them a certain level of embarrassment. Skills I have yet to master.

Fast forward to the present day. No longer does coach keep anything from me. Or me from anything. He throws it all at me. Double-unders. Rope climbs. Chest-to-bar pull-ups. Overhead squats. Thirty-inch box jumps. Toes to bar. Handstand push-ups. Wall climbs. Parachute runs. Sled drags. Skier.

In fact, every day this week, something new. Workouts that take two hours to complete. Workouts that leave me finishing well after everyone else has gone home. Workouts that break my routine. And, just as I finished writing this, the boy added something completely new to today's workout.

Maybe, just maybe, you can teach an old dog new tricks.

This is the moral of the story: It is okay to live within your habits. Just be sure they do not house your excuses.

August 18

Why you so chill?
—Youmna El Kabaili

This is an open letter.

To a child. To your child. To the child in you.

Dear Child,

In life, there is not much I can control. I possess not the power over big things. Like the words and actions of others. Or even little things, like the weather.

I possess not the foresight to plan for unseen events that suddenly unfold. Nor do I know when a crisis shall arise.

In life, there is not much I can bend to my will. Time, I cannot alter. Yesterday, I cannot change. Tomorrow, I cannot predict.

I possess neither the strength nor the desire to change nouns. People. Places. Things.

In life, there is not much I can impact. The footprint I leave, soon gone. The ripple I make, soon calm. The light I shine, soon dimmed.

But in life, there is always one thing I possess. One thing I control. One thing I can bend, change, alter. One thing I have that leaves a lasting imprint: my attitude.

By choosing my attitude, I give myself the greatest power I will need in life. The power to control me. My words. My actions. My approach to a crisis.

By choosing my attitude, I possess the strength I need to change the only thing I should ever focus on changing...me.

By choosing my attitude, I may leave an imprint of permanence on my small corner of the world. Perhaps my ripple will become a wave. And maybe, just maybe, another will pick up the torch.

Love,

Me

August 19

Personal power is the ability to stand on your own two feet with a smile on your face in the middle of a universe that contains a million ways to crush you.
—J. Z. Colby

This is your pep talk.

Power through
Stumble through
You are not through

Stand up
Reach up
You are up to this

Find a way
Light the way
You are the way

Trust your path
Follow your own path
You are on the right path

Value what matters
Prioritize what matters
You are what matters

Fight the fear
Fight the excuses
You are worth the fight

Honor the dream within
Nurture the dream given you
You are the dream

You've just been pep-talked.

August 20

I don't understand how I can know so little about love and how it works. How I can be so bad at it when it's all I've ever wanted. All I've ever known is about leaving or being left.
—Carrie Ryan

You are leaving. Slowly slipping away.

I shall not cling to you. But forever I will hold you close in my heart and memory.

You are leaving. Slowly fading from view.

I shall not search for you. But always will I see you amongst my dreams.

You are leaving. Slowly passing from my tomorrows.

But beautifully you left an imprint on my yesterdays.

You are leaving. Slowly going your own way.

But you provided a light for me to follow.

You are leaving. Slowly leaving me to carry on.

But you gifted me a set of wings so I may soar.

You are leaving. But you will never be gone.

For you are ever a part of me.

Hugs, prayers, love.

August 21

Does the walker choose the path, or the path the walker?
—Garth Nix

This is a story.

I may be taken from my path of comfort, but it will not keep me from moving forward. I am growing.

I may be taken down a path more challenging, but it will not stop me from reaching my destination. I am unstoppable.

I may be taken down a path unfamiliar, but it will not cause me to doubt my steps. I am confident.

I may be taken down a path less traveled, but it will not lead me away from my truth. I am certain of my place.

I may be taken down a path others cannot see, but it will not cause me to fear. I am courage.

I may be taken down a path hoping to defeat me, but it will not bring me to my knees. I am strong.

I may be taken down a path I never saw coming, but it will not alter my faith. I believe.

I may be taken down a path filled with heartache, but it will not change the love I know. I am unwavering.

This is the moral of the story: The path does not determine me. I shall remain true to me, no matter where I wander.

August 22

You are growing into consciousness, and my wish for you is that you feel
no need to constrict yourself to make other people comfortable.
—Ta-Nehisi Coates

I have to stop apologizing for being me. For those who cannot handle my fire, my drive, my intensity, my jagged edges. My rough spots merely broken pieces that may never heal. They will not harm you.

I have to stop hiding me. For those who may fear my light, my gifts, my vastness, my confidence. My shine does not dull your brilliance. It should not frighten you.

I have to stop discounting me. For those who do not value my wants, my needs, my path, my worth. My worth never exceeds or diminishes yours. Know your value.

I have to stop playing the small me. For those who would minimize the size of my goals, my courage, my successes, my heart. My growth propels me forward. It will not impede yours.

I have to stop explaining me. For those who do not understand my passions, my desires, my love, my dreams. These are my life's interpretive dance. If you cannot hear my song, do not judge.

I have to be me. For me.

August 23

Sometimes the darkest challenges, the most difficult
lessons, hold the greatest gems of light.
—Barbara Marciniak

I am being challenged. Made to face longstanding fears.

Made to rethink the view I hold of myself.

I am being challenged. On a journey others do not understand.

On a path I cannot always see.

I am being challenged. Earning bruises.

Earning strength.

I am being challenged. To move to a place of discomfort.

To reach my limitless.

I am being challenged. Some pieces broken.

Some pieces no longer fit.

I am being challenged. Chiseling the stone.

Shaping my dream.

I am being challenged. To discover who will show up when the challenge seems too great.

To discover the hero in me.

I am being challenged. And I welcome this gift.

August 24

You are your own hero. Do not wait for someone to save you,
rescue you or tell you that you are ok. Be the hero of your own
story and never, ever let them make you the victim.
—John Goode

Alone with my darkness
Patiently waited
For another to light a way for me
No one arrived

Alone with my fears
Patiently waited
For another to fight for me
No one arrived

Alone with my regrets
Patiently waited
For another to forgive me
No one arrived

Alone with my brokenness
Patiently waited
For another to save me
No one arrived

Alone with my life
Waited no more
No one was coming
Became my own hero.

August 25

Being good is making it look easy, but getting good is never easy.
—Jeffrey Fry

I've been told, "You make it look easy."

Here's the truth. My easy came hard.

Doing the status quo is easy.
Accepting change is hard.
My easy came hard.

Quitting is easy.
Continuing when the pain arrives is hard.
My easy came hard.

Making excuses is easy.
Rising above what I believe limits me is hard.
My easy came hard.

Standing still is easy.
Pushing. Reaching. Striving. Taking the leap. This is hard.
My easy came hard.

Playing it safe is easy.
Having the courage to do what must be done is hard.
My easy came hard.

Wishing is easy.
Relentlessly pursuing a dream is hard.
My easy came hard.

August 26

The world is surely wide enough to walk without fear.
—Jeanette Winterson

I am walking into the unknown.
Without fear.
For I am free to find my answers.

I am walking toward the void.
Without fear.
For I am filled with hope.

I am walking amongst the shadows.
Without fear.
For I am my own source of light.

I am walking beyond the horizon.
Without fear.
For I know something awaits me there.

I am walking nearer the ledge.
Without fear.
For I have learned to trust my wings.

I am walking on. Without fear.

August 27

Non sum qualis eram. I am not what I once was.
—*Francesca Lia Block*

The change in me came slowly. Almost imperceptibly.

It could not be measured in standard terms.
Not in pounds or inches.
Not by time or distance.

As water carves the stone.
As time weathers the earth.
As seasons pass into years.

The change in me came slowly. Imperceptibly. Yet inevitably.

For I am not who I once was.
No longer defined by a past that does not fit me.
No longer shaped by that which does not serve my good.

For I am not who I once was.
No longer fearful of my light.
No longer a stranger to my gifts.

For I am not who I once was.
No longer willing to settle.
No longer standing still.

The change in me came slowly. Imperceptibly. Inevitably.

August 28

When you are loved, you can do anything in creation. When you are loved, there's no need at all to understand what's happening, because everything happens within you.
—Paulo Coelho

This is a story.

On endurance: You can go on

On strength: You have enough

On failing: You will be okay

On excuses: You do not need those

On fears: You are greater

On happiness: You can choose this

On dreams: You have waited long enough

On choice: You will make the right ones

On worth: You do matter

On faith: You are hope-filled

On doubt: You can let it go

On blessings: You have many

On standing: You will rise again

On discipline: You do what needs done

On love: You are loved

This is the moral of the story: You can. You have. You will. You do. You are.

August 29

I'm not an artist
How then shall I see beauty
Given but two eyes

I'm not a poet
How then shall I win your heart
When left but speechless

I'm not an actor
How then shall I know my lines
Living unrehearsed

I'm not a psychic
How then shall I be ready
My fortune untold

I'm not a machine
How then shall I not collapse
Feeling all the pain

I'm not a hero
How then shall I save a life
Without a red cape

I'm not an angel
How then shall I ever soar
With wings so fragile

I'm but a human
How shall I ever be loved
Being imperfect.

August 30

You want help? Ask for help. You want love? Ask for love. If you want anything from the universe, anything from yourself, you must first ask.
—Kamand Kojouri

For a child. For your child. For the child in you.

As a parent and teacher, I get asked a lot of questions and for a lot of things.

If I could speak to the children, here are the most important things I would tell them to ask.

1. Ask for what you need more than for what you want: Learn the difference.

2. Ask to earn what you want: Expect no handouts. Do the hard work.

3. Ask for a chance to make amends: You will mess up. You will make mistakes. Make it right.

4. Ask for forgiveness: See #3.

5. Ask, "What can I do to help?": If you simply approach problems from this perspective, much is solved.

6. Ask for help when needed: This is not weakness. We all need help from others from time to time.

7. Ask to be respected, not liked: Being popular is fleeting. It depends on the whims of others. Being respected is foundational. It depends on *your* actions.

8. Ask to be challenged: Not by others, but by yourself. Raise your own bar.

9. Ask not for easy but for strength: The easy path rarely takes you where you need to go. Strength allows you to travel any road.

10. Ask, "How can I make a difference?" It is your one true purpose.

August 31

When we honestly ask ourselves which person in our lives mean the most to us, we often find that it is those who, instead of giving advice, solutions, or cures, have chosen rather to share our pain and touch our wounds with a warm and tender hand. The friend who can be silent with us in a moment of despair or confusion, who can stay with us in an hour of grief and bereavement, who can tolerate not knowing, not curing, not healing and face with us the reality of our powerlessness, that is a friend who cares.
—Henri J. M. Nouwen

Dear Friend,

I do not know all your pain
But I feel the hurt in you
Because I am your friend

I do not know your ghosts
But I feel the haunting in you
Because I am your friend

I do not know your tears
But I feel the silent cry in you
Because I am your friend

I do not know your loss
But I feel the emptiness in you
Because I am your friend

I do not know your brokenness
But I feel the jagged edges in you
Because I am your friend

I do not know the words to say
But because I am your friend
I hope you feel my love in you.

Love,

Me

September 1

Your power to choose can never be taken from you. It can be neglected and it can be ignored. But if used, it can make all the difference.
—Steve Goodier

If you could choose your path, do not seek the shortcut.

If you could choose your story, do not allow another to write it.

If you could choose your worth, do not let anyone diminish it.

If you could choose your light, do not ever hide from it.

If you could choose your words, do not forget to speak from a place of kindness, humility, love.

If you could choose your blessings, do not count from a place of wanting.

If you could choose your gifts, do not forget to know gratitude.

If you could choose your dream, do not dream small.

If you could choose your legacy, do not doubt you make a difference.

If you could choose your love, do not settle for one of convenience.

Do not forget: you always get to choose.

September 2

The bird dares to break the shell, then the shell breaks open and the bird can fly openly. This is the simplest principle of success. You dream, you dare and you fly.
—Israelmore Ayivor

This is a story.

You can wish for easy, or you can work to make your hard easy.

You can hope to finish, or you can prepare to finish.

You can be afraid of failing and do nothing, or you can see that failing is nothing to be afraid of.

You can break the promises you made to yourself, or you can promise yourself you will not break.

You can believe you are not strong enough, or you can be strong enough to believe in you.

You can make excuses for not chasing your passion, or your passion can be an excuse for what you're chasing.

You can dream of the life you want to live, or you can live the dream for your life.

This is the moral of the story: either way, you *can*.

September 3

I believe in love. I believe in hard times and love winning. I believe marriage is hard. I believe people make mistakes. I believe people can want two things at once. I believe people are selfish and generous at the same time. I believe very few people want to hurt others. I believe that you can be surprised by life. I believe in happy endings.
—Isabel Gillies

I still believe in...

...hope's power

...faith's light

...love's eternal flame

...humanity's goodness

...yesterday's lessons

...today's message

...tomorrow's promise

...giving unselfishly

...gifts of the heart

...doing right

...forgiving wrongs

...goose bumps

...chasing unicorns

...dreams coming true

...the broken road

...a place called home

...love unwavering

I simply still believe.

September 4

Today is a day, like every other day, brimming with possibility. A day to treat
people with kindness and respect. A day to move closer to fulfilling your dreams.
A day to forgive yourself for absolutely everything. A day to smile with gratitude.
Today is a day, like every other day, to create the kind of life
you want to live, the kind that makes you feel good and right,
the kind of life you were born to realize. Today.
—Scott Stabile

Today does not look back at yesterday with regret, or forward to tomorrow with worry.

It exists in the present.

Today holds all the light and promise and hope it needs.

It is complete.

Today fears neither the storms on the horizon nor the gathering clouds.

It is prepared for the storm.

Today understands it has been given only so much time to fulfill its destiny.

It wastes no time in doing so.

Today cares not of words spoken or perceptions long held.

It simply shows up and unfolds its truth.

Today contains within in it untold stories, unknown glories, untapped potential.

It seeks to know them.

Today is beauty and life and love all rolled into this simple and amazing package.

It is a gift.

Things to do: be like today.

September 5

They handed me a new set of keys
To doors I've never walked through
To locks I've never dared remove
And my hands slowly trembled

They handed me a new set of keys
To gates that held me for so long
Daring me to finally free myself
And my hands slowly trembled

They handed me a new set of keys
To the dungeon of my darkness
And asked me to step into the light
And my hands slowly trembled

They handed me a new set of keys
But I've always known the truth
The trembling of my hands
Was merely my heart overflowing.

September 6

Your life is like a coin. You can spend it anyway you want, but
only once. Make sure you invest it and don't waste it. Invest it in
something that matters to you and matters for eternity.
—Tony Evens

It matters not how far you go,
So long as you travel beyond your comfort zone.

It matters not how strong you feel,
So long as you move past your point of weakness.

It matters not how fast you go,
So long as you outrun the voices of doubt.

It matters not who you best,
So long as you push yourself to be better.

It matters not when or how you finish,
So long as you do not quit.

What matters most is that it mattered enough for you to go.

September 7

It is a big world, full of things that steal your breath and fill
your belly with fire...But where you go when you leave isn't as
important as where you go when you come home.
—Lindsay Eagar

Taking the long way home
On this endless roam
Hoping I may one day find
Tranquility and peace of mind.

With each rising of the sun
More miles must be run
Another day in the journey
The search to simply be.

So again this day I set out
Filled with wonder, filled with doubt
About where my road may lead
But as I wander I am freed.

Where I've been cannot stay
Though I do not know the way
I take comfort as I roam
For I am one day closer to home.

September 8

I guess everyone has a bird urge when they look down heights, a desire to jump,
without wing or buoyant sail. Fear of heights is fear of a desire to jump.
—Amruta Patil

You stood at the very edge of healing
But fear made you feel broken
And so you dared not jump
Never knowing you are permitted
To finally allow yourself to be okay.

You stood at the very edge of change
But fear made you cling to the past
And so you dared not jump
Never knowing letting loose that chain
Will allow you to truly soar.

You stood at the very edge of magic
But fear made the net invisible
And so you dared not jump
Never knowing the magic occurs
When you believe you will be caught.

You stood at the very edge of love
But fear made you question it
And so you dared not jump
Never knowing your heart knows
This love was the answer you sought.

You stand at the very edge of your life.
Something amazing awaits
Just beyond the edge of fear
Healing. Change. Magic. Love.
Dare to jump.

September 9

Not always sure where I'm supposed to be
The path ahead cannot always see.

Not always sure where I'm supposed to go
Answers to my questions don't always know.

Not always sure where I'm supposed to land
Life has not always gone as planned.

Not always sure where my path runs out
Steps often filled with doubt.

Not always sure where is my next destination
Seems I'm always trying to find my location.

Not always sure where I'm going
But then comes a simple knowing.

And this has set me free
I am right where I am supposed to be.

September 10

Though we may not have reached the heights we anticipated
yesterday, today is a brand new day to begin a new climb.
—Chinonye J. Chidolue

I am reaching new heights
For I simply keep climbing

I am reaching new heights
For I now trust my strength

I am reaching new heights
For I am constantly looking up

I am reaching new heights
For I relentlessly reach higher

I am reaching new heights
For I believe in my wings

I am reaching new heights
For I no longer fear the fall.

September 11

To live, to TRULY live, we must be willing to RISK. To be nothing
in order to find everything. To leap before we look.
—Mandy Hale

Sometimes.
I challenge myself.

Sometimes.
I chase ghosts.

Sometimes.
I bleed.

Sometimes.
I force myself out of idle.

Sometimes.
I seek my wall.

Sometimes.
I push past my limits.

Sometimes.
I neglect the impossible.

Sometimes.
I truly live.

September 12

Perhaps I am broken, he conceded silently, but broken bones
heal stronger, and I will have my day in the sun.
—Peter V. Brett

I am getting stronger.
Stronger than my excuses.

I am getting stronger.
Stronger than my can't.

I am getting stronger.
Stronger than my fears.

I am getting stronger.
Stronger than my doubts.

I am getting stronger.
Stronger than my weak.

I am getting stronger.
Stronger than my yesterday.

Today, I will get stronger.

September 13

I dwell in possibility...
—Emily Dickinson

I believe:

In the possibilities

Boundaries are not permanent

Fear is not a stop sign

Hope is endless

Discipline trumps motivation

Failing offers lessons

Faith lights the lamp

Trust leads the way

Gratitude multiplies blessings

A dream is a destination

Love is the greatest force

September 14

*Do not undervalue what you are ultimately worth because
you are at a momentary disadvantage.*
—Sherry Thomas

Dear you,

I heard you say, "I have so many excuses."

You have not a list of excuses. You have a number of obstacles.

Still needing to be overcome. Still waiting for you to rise above. Still chances to grow stronger. Still just another part of living.

I heard you say, "I am so very tired."

You have not given up. You have a reason to rest.

Still, you must get up. Still, you will rise again. Still, you cannot remain here. Still, there is work to be done.

I heard you say, "I feel like I have failed."

You have not failed. You have learned lessons.

Still, it may feel like failure. Still, it may require starting over. Still, it may be frustrating. Still, it is not failing if you try again.

I heard you say, "I have lost all heart."

You have not lost heart. You have a heart.

Still beating. Still capable of falling in love. Still fighting for you. Still doing the work of living.

How then do you overcome all that I have heard you say?

You simply say, "Still, I am worth it."

Love,

Me

September 15

Everything we do, we do for love. The beauty of love is that in giving it away, you are left with more than you had before.
—David Simon

Dear Love,

For you, I would venture miles untold.

For you, I would choose the difficult path.

For you, I would awake before the dawn.

For you, I would forgo sleep.

For you, I would chase a waking dream.

For you, I would suffer heartache.

For you, I would allow my heart to race.

For you, I would seek out goose bumps.

For you, I would raise my bar.

For you, I would better myself.

For you, I would alter my life.

For you, I would make no excuses.

For you, I would commit unwaveringly.

I would. For you.

Love,

Me

September 16

Our life is our masterpiece, it's up to us on how we paint our story. It's up to us how we see the substances we have. At the end of the day, all our accumulated stuff will be presented as our greatest piece of work.
—Nathaniel E. Quimada

You've been given a blank canvas.
To paint your picture.
To tell your story.
To splash your name upon.
It's called today.

You've been given yet another chance.
To try again.
To get it right.
To start all over if you must.
It's called today.

You've been given a stepping stone.
To move you forward.
To help you progress.
To construct your path.
It's called today.

You've been given a gift so precious and rare.
To tear into.
To completely unwrap.
To possess for but a time.
It's called today.

You've been given a finite amount of time.
To spend as you wish.
To fully cherish.
To make memories from.
It's called today.

You've been given the foundation for your future success.
To build upon.
To invest in.
To launch yourself from.
It's called today.

Today—it's calling.

September 17

That was the thing about the world: it wasn't that things
were harder than you thought they were going to be, it was
that they were hard in ways that you didn't expect.
—Lev Grossman

For a child. For your child. For the child in you.

Dear Child,

If you think succeeding is difficult, try quitting. See just how difficult life becomes when you learn to quit. When you quit on something. A dream. When you quit on someone. Yourself.

If you think being yourself is difficult, try being someone else. See just how difficult life becomes when you are not true to yourself. When you pretend to be someone you are not. When you do not honor your true self.

If you think being thankful is difficult, try being ungrateful. See just how difficult life becomes when you do not express gratitude for the blessings you have. When you fail to recognize the gifts you receive. When you do not say, "Thank you."

If you think being loved and loving is difficult, try not opening your heart to love. See just how difficult life becomes when you close yourself off to those who love you. When you choose anger over forgiveness. When you choose not to give love a chance.

Life is difficult enough. Do not quit. Be yourself. Express gratitude. Choose love.

Love,

Me

September 18

Sometimes, the simplest and hardest thing to say is, "I am sorry."

Sometimes, the simplest and hardest thing to say is, "I forgive you."

Sometimes, the simplest and hardest thing to say is, "I love you."

Sometimes, the simplest and hardest thing to say is, "I need help."

Sometimes, the simplest and hardest thing to say is, "I need to make a change."

Sometimes, the simplest and hardest thing to say is, "I miss you."

Sometimes, the simplest and hardest thing to say is, "I will be okay."

Sometimes, simple or hard, you must say what you need to say.

September 19

What you have always believed in is the real you.
—Tapan Ghosh

It is not that I think I can fly.

It is that I believe in my ability to relentlessly launch myself forward.

It is not that I think I do not have weaknesses.

It is that I believe they are merely markers to help me find my strength.

It is not that I think I am invincible.

It is that I believe I am always capable of rising after a fall.

It is not that I think I am super.

It is that I believe I possess gifts unique to me.

It is not that I think I can save the world.

It is that I believe I am powerful enough to change mine.

It is not that I think I am more than human.

It is that I believe my humanness is more than enough.

It is not that I think. It is that I believe. And *that* is the key.

September 20

This is an open letter.

Dear Friend,

I believe in your light. The one you try to hide. The one you fear letting others see. The one you often deny. I believe in your light. For it has lit my once darkened path.

I believe in your capacity to endure. The heartache and sadness. The grief and the loss. The uncertainty and the struggles. I believe in your capacity to endure. For it has taught me I can go on.

I believe in your strength. The quiet determination. The doing each day what you are able to do. The resolve to once more pick yourself up. I believe in your strength. For it has shown me I am stronger than I know.

I believe in your journey. The miles you felt lost. The steps you took even as you trembled. The broken road you have traveled upon. I believe in your journey. For it has given me hope as I set out on mine.

I believe in you. And you have given me reason to believe in me.

Love,

Me

September 21

This is a story.

It has been a long-held theory that anything that has risen must eventually fall.

And my life has seemingly been a testament to this theory. I, its living proof.

So many times have I been lifted up, only to fall so hard. The proof is in my scars.

So many times have I been to the mountaintop, only to find myself in the valley below. The proof is in my continued climb.

So many times have I been able to spread my wings and soar, only to have them clipped. The proof is in my fear of falling.

So many times have I been on cloud nine, only to have my parade rained upon. The proof is in my tears.

So many times have I been so close to love, only to watch it disappear. The proof is in my broken heart.

And yet, perhaps we have the theory all wrong. You see, after each fall, I have always risen. Each and every single time.

Perhaps cautiously, but always willing to try again.

Perhaps foolishly, but always wiser.

Perhaps anxiously, but always hope-filled.

Perhaps slowly, but always stronger.

This is the moral of the story: What falls must again rise. For I, its living proof.

September 22

The best thing about the future is that it only comes one day at a time.
—Abraham Lincoln

Today, I do not have to cover all the miles of the future.

Today, I do not have to answer all the questions of the future.

Today, I do not have to stress over the unknowns of the future.

Today, I do not have to reach the destination of the future.

Today, I do not have to solve all the problems of the future.

Today, I do not have to achieve the dream of the future.

Today, I do not have to be the me of the future.

Today, I do not have to fear the future.

Today, I simply have to do today.

This, all the future ever depends upon.

September 23

But remember, nothing comes without a price. Our
paths are not mapped; they're made.
—*Priya Ardis*

This is a story.

Each day, I add to the path
To where I hope to be
To where I want to be
To where I plan to be

Each day, I add to the path
Humbly
Carefully
Surely

Each day, I add to the path
A labor of love
A work of art
A step forward

Each day, I add to the path
Little by little
Step by step
Piece by piece

Each day, I add to the path
From a place of trust
From a place of resilience
From a place of strength

Each day, I add to the path
Of my story
Of my dream
Of my life

Each day, I add to the path
With patience
With faith
With love

This is the moral of the story: each day I add to the path, I am that much further along.

September 24

The only way that we can live, is if we grow. The only way that we can grow is if we change. The only way that we can change is if we learn. The only way we can learn is if we are exposed. And the only way that we can become exposed is if we throw ourselves out into the open. Do it. Throw yourself.
—C. JoyBell C.

Ten life lessons learned on growing and changing:

1. Strength is a reservoir you must repeatedly dip yourself into.

2. You are not guaranteed things will be easy; you are simply afforded an opportunity to grow.

3. Dreams require discipline. Discipline requires consistency. Consistency requires intention. Intention requires choice. Thus, achieving your dream comes down to the choices you make.

4. Change is only going to happen when ingrained patterns, habits, beliefs, and perceptions are altered.

5. If change is going to happen, you cannot fear changing.

6. Fear does not have a grip on you. You have a grip on fear. When you are ready, let it go.

7. Ultimately, your choices or your excuses will construct the path you walk. See #3.

8. There are no shortcuts. There is persistence. There is patience. Anything else is cheating yourself or someone trying to sell you something.

9. Struggling does not mean failure. Difficult does not mean impossible. It often means you need to grow into something. See #2.

10. Most of what I have yet to accomplish, I already believe I can accomplish.

September 25

Our infinitesimal hopes should survive longer than our vast disappointments.
—Munia Khan

If you should doubt
Doubt the doubters
Doubt the notion of impossible
Doubt the whisper of "I can't"

If you should worry
Worry small
Worry less, trust more
Worry with faith

If you should quit
Quit settling
Quit discounting yourself
Quit accepting less

If you should give up
Give up doubting
Give up worrying
Give up quitting

If you should wander
Wander past your limits
Wander to the other side of fear
Wander toward your dreams

If you should get lost
Get lost inside your hopes
Get lost amongst your dreams
Get lost beyond your comfort

If you should fall
Fall forward
Fall with wings spread
Fall completely in love

If you should fear
Fear never wandering
Fear never getting lost
Fear never falling.

September 26

Success begins at the extra mile.
—*Yuikan Shirik*

You know you don't have to go the extra mile.

You know you don't have to hit the road again today.

You know you don't have to do another set.

You know you don't have to go beyond your comfort zone.

You know you don't have to face your fears.

You know you don't have to be better than yesterday.

You know you don't have to get in another rep.

You know you don't have to run that hill.

You know you don't have to keep pushing.

You know you don't have to accept the challenge.

You know you don't have to. You get to.

September 27

*Life is about accepting the challenges along the way, choosing
to keep moving forward, and savoring the journey.*
—Roy T. Bennett

Ten life lessons learned on falling, moving, and traveling your path:

1. Life is all about finding a way to stay upright, despite the occasional stumble and constant pull of gravity.

2. If you fall, get up, dust yourself off, take a moment to tuck yourself in, and then get back to moving.

3. The sharp pains to your sole (or soul) are life's way of telling you not to remain in this place.

4. Do not look too far ahead.

5. The very next step determines whether you fall or whether you keep moving forward. Choose wisely.

6. In life, there are perceived dangers and actual dangers. Do not let fear determine your path.

7. You can wish for the easy path or you can prepare for the one that will challenge you

8. The easy path rarely leads to the mountaintop.

9. Life is hard. But the ride is beautiful.

10. It is not always about running through life, but rather, bounding joyfully through it.

September 28

I have mastered the art of smiling.
But there are times the tears still fall.
I am a work in progress.

I have mastered my fears.
But there are nights they lie down beside me.
I am a work in progress.

I have mastered the past.
But there are days it stares right back at me.
I am a work in progress.

I have mastered flight.
But there are moments it feels as if I am free-falling.
I am a work in progress.

I have mastered the voices in my head.
But there are whispers that still haunt me.
I am a work in progress.

I have mastered the tests put before me.
But there are questions I have yet to answer.
I am a work in progress.

I have mastered the path I am walking.
But there are steps still so difficult to take.
I am a work in progress.

There is much I have mastered. There is much progress yet to make.

September 29

Your prayer for someone may or may not change them, but it always changes YOU.
—*Craig Groeschel*

Dear Friend,

Tonight, my prayers shall be for you.

May sleep find you gently.

May peace of mind be your companion.

May worries not dwell in your heart.

May comfort settle over you.

May your pains and burdens fall away.

May you deeply rest.

May a quiet come to your mind.

May dreams carry you forward.

May you feel my love.

This, I pray for you.

September 30

But there was a special kind of gift that came with embracing the chaos, even if I cursed most of the way. I'm convinced that, when everything is wiped blank, it's life's way of forcing you to become acquainted with and aware of who you are now, who you can become. What is the fulfillment of your soul?
—Jennifer DeLucy

What will it be that causes your soul to be stirred to action?

What will it be that causes your fears to be set aside?

What will it be that causes your worry to dissipate?

What will it be that causes your breath to be taken away?

What will it be that causes your wings to be unfurled?

What will it be that causes your smile to be shared?

What will it be that causes your spirit to know goose bumps?

What will it be that causes your heart to race?

What will it be that causes your life to be inspired?

Do more of that.

October 1

Your life is the proof that beauty can still be attained.
—Lana M. H. Wilder

Advice on life, from a pair of running shoes.

It's messy out there; be careful.

Your path, no other may walk.

It's a bumpy ride; lace 'em up tight.

When you get hurt, rub a little dirt on it, pick yourself up, and keep moving.

It's not about style points, it's about substance.

Tread lightly, but leave a lasting impression.

Where you end up depends upon the direction you set yourself toward.

Let your soul guide you.

Make sure it is a good fit for you, but allow room for growth.

One size does not fit all.

It isn't always pretty, but it is always beautiful.

October 2

The answer to every adversity lies in courageously moving forward with faith.
—Edmond Mbiaka

There Is No Shame: There is no shame in walking. There is no shame in selecting a pace that allows you to be successful. There is no shame. What there is, is strength and grace in finding a way to move continually forward.

Remember Your Strengths: So many times it seems we hold back. Never fully using or displaying our light, our talents, our strengths. Perhaps out of fear of what others might think. Perhaps humility. Perhaps we do not trust our self. You possess a unique light. Shine it. We are all made better for it. You have developed so many talents. Through trial and error. Through living a life filled with challenges. Use them. You have strengths. Play to them. Remember them.

Remain Humble: One of my favorite lines, from one of my favorite poems, reads as follows. "If you compare yourself with others, you may become vain and bitter; for always there will be greater and lesser persons than yourself. Enjoy your achievements as well as your plans." In other words. Remain humble. Run your race. Live your life. Avoid comparisons. Be you. That is good enough. Always.

Stay Level: Life does that sometimes. You are given a challenge to overcome. You do. And you are feeling good. Then, it throws another challenge at you. And then another. And the overall effect is that no matter how small the challenge, it begins to wear you down. And you just want life to level out. But here is the lesson. Life won't. You are the one who must stay level. Keep your head about you. Know you have gotten through all the climbs. Know you will again. And as the road rises again before you, you are strong enough to get over it.

Power Through: We all struggle. Often with the same problems. Work. Relationships. Family. The many to do's. And yet, there are those who seem to power through them. No whining. No drama. No stopping. No complaining or cursing their lot in life. They simply and quietly put their head down, and go about using their strength to overcome the struggle. Be like that. Power through.

Conserve Your Energy: Truth is, we all only have so much energy to go around. But we often let worry and stress and fear steal so much of our energy. We invest energy in those things we cannot control. You must decide what is important to you. Establish your priories. Then, invest your energy there. Conserve your energy for your passions, your dreams, your loves. Do not waste energy on the trivial. The small. These are not your finish lines. And, the more energy you invest here, the less you will have for what is really important in your life.

Fight for your Finish: Life does that. It wants to know your priorities. Your passions. Your dreams. Your loves. And then, it tests you to see exactly how bad you want them. Are you willing to fight for them? And, you have to. Kick and scream and cry, if you must, but fight for them. Fight to make your impossible a lie. Fight to make your dreams a tangible reality. Fight for what you love. Fight for your finish.

October 3

Remember, you see in any situation what you expect to see.
—David J. Schwartz

Perhaps we have been looking at things from the wrong perspective.

Fear does not have you. You have fear.
Thus, you are the one in control of it.

Happiness does not find you. You find happiness.
Thus, you are the one in control of where to look for it.

Comfort does not become you. You become comfortable.
Thus, you are the one in control of moving beyond your comfort zone.

Excuses do not own you. You own your excuses.
Thus, you are the one in control of whether or not you will use them.

Faith does not question you. You question your faith.
Thus, you are the one in control of what you choose to believe.

Strength does not fail you. You fail to recognize your own strength.
Thus, you are the one in control of deciding you are indeed strong enough.

Another does not have power over you. You give away your power to another.
Thus, you are the one in control of taking it back.

Hope does not choose you as the vessel. You choose hope as your vessel.
Thus, you are the one in control of living hope-filled.

Life does not place value upon you. You place value upon your life.
Thus, you are the one in control of determining your worth.

Perhaps, if we change our perspective, we can begin to see: we control so much of what we have in life.

October 4

Something always comes to fill the empty spaces and this is
what I've come to do with white space. I invite thanks.
—Ann Voskamp

This is a story.

There is a space between need and want. When it is filled with gratitude, you will find you have more than enough.

There is a space between now and yet. When it is filled with patience, you will find you are where you belong.

There is a space between doubt and trust. When it is filled with acceptance, you will find the absence of fear.

There is a space between despair and hope. When it is filled with faith, you will find a reason to believe.

There is a space between discord and harmony. When it is filled with forgiveness, you will find peace.

There is a space between waking and sleeping. When it is filled with love, you will find your purpose for living.

This is the moral of the story: There are spaces within you needing to be filled. When you fill them with good, you will find what you are looking for.

October 5

They may not have enough of their own to take a stand,
but they can do it if someone shows them how.
—Dan Groat

This is a story.

In the distance, my mountain awaits.
But here where I stand today, I shall gather my strength.

In the distance, storms clouds build.
But here where I stand today, I shall prepare my shelter.

In the distance, shadows and darkness appear.
But here where I stand today, I shall fan my flames.

In the distance, fears begin to form.
But here where I stand today, I shall summon my courage.

In the distance, the road takes unknown turns.
But here where I stand today, I shall map my course.

In the distance, doubts grow in number.
But here where I stand today, I shall fill myself with faith.

In the distance, many questions arise.
But here where I stand today, I shall find my answers.

This is the moral of the story: Take a stand. Here. Today. You will be ready to go the distance.

October 6

Happiness is a warm puppy.
—Charles M. Schulz

Happiness is:

An easy Sunday morning

An easy run

The sounds of quiet

The sounds of laughter

A good book

A good friend

Time to reflect

Time to simply be

A warm blanket

A warm smile

A dream being chased

A dream fulfilled

The gift of giving

The gift of gratitude

Free to share

Free to all

A prayer answered

A prayer for you

Within reach

Within you

October 7

The strength of your mind determines the quality of your life.
—Edmond Mbiaka

Physically you can, when mentally you stop saying you can't.

Physically you accept the burden, when mentally you are not burdened by negative thoughts.

Physically you rise, when mentally you see yourself getting up.

Physically you endure, when mentally you do not tire.

Physically you overcome, when mentally you prepare for the challenge.

Physically you grow stronger, when mentally you focus on your strengths.

Physically you move beyond the wall, when mentally you envision no limits.

Physically you succeed, when mentally you understand, you will not fail.

Physically you do, when mentally you believe.

October 8

The compass rose is nothing but a star with an infinite
number of rays pointing in all directions.
It is the one true and perfect symbol of the universe. And it is the one most
accurate symbol of you. Spread your arms in an embrace, throw your
head back, and prepare to receive and send coordinates of being. For, at
last you know—you are the navigator, the captain, and the ship.
—Vera Nazarian

Seven irrefutable facts—one for each day of this week. Take in small doses. Digest slowly.

1. Until you move toward what you want, nothing will get different. Action begets change.

2. Your choices always determine your results. Hence, if you do not get what you want, choose more carefully.

3. The power of discipline outlasts the whim of motivation. Therefore, losing your motivation is an invalid excuse.

4. What you are able to do matters much more than what you are unable to do. But what you *decide* to do matters even more.

5. You were given wings for a reason. You do not honor your gift if you never test your ability to soar.

6. Your path. If it isn't where you want to go, choose a different direction. You are the captain.

7. Your story. If you don't like the script, rewrite it. You are the author.

October 9

The path to our destination is not always a straight one. We go down the wrong road, we get lost, we turn back. Maybe it doesn't matter which road we embark on. Maybe what matters is that we embark.
—Barbara Hall

My path is rarely easy
For I have known the darkness
It holds all my fears
At times it has filled my soul

My path is rarely clear
For I have known obstacles
They hold all my weaknesses
At times they seem insurmountable

My path is rarely marked
For I have known dead ends
They hold all my loneliness
At times they appear at every turn

My path is rarely safe
For I have known brokenness
It holds all I have ever lost
At times it consumes me

My path, I shall continue traveling
For I know something awaits me
It holds all I have ever dreamed of
And in time, I shall arrive.

October 10

Some broken vases can still hold beautiful flowers.
—Munia Khan

I am still learning
Through the trials and stumbles
Through the missteps and mistakes
I am still learning

I am still trying
Despite the bruises and scars
Despite the setbacks and unknowns
I am still trying

I am still fighting
For my strength to be realized
For my place to stand
I am still fighting

I am still becoming
The me I hope to be
The me I am worthy of
I am still becoming

I am still growing
Beyond the limits of my fears
Beyond the comfort of my excuses
I am still growing

I am still dreaming
Of the truths I hold closest
Of one day coming home
I am still dreaming

I am still unwavering
In the love I have to offer
In the love I hope to know
I am still unwavering

I am. Still.

October 11

I meet people and they become chapters in my stories.
—Avijeet Das

We shall meet along the road, my friend. And we shall share a story. You and I.

We shall not speak of how many miles you covered. For in your story, I shall come to understand how far you have journeyed.

We shall meet along the road, my friend. And we shall share a story. You and I.

We shall not speak of how you arrived here. For in your story, I shall come to understand how you have made your way to this place.

We shall meet along the road, my friend. And we shall share a story. You and I.

We shall not speak of weaknesses or failures. For in your story, I shall come to understand how your strength moves you forward.

We shall meet along the road, my friend. And we shall share a story. You and I.

We shall not speak of hopelessness or regrets. For in your story, I shall come to understand all you still dream of.

We shall meet along the road, my friend.

We shall share a story.

And we shall come to understand, we are now a part of the same story.

You and I.

October 12

*There is some kind of a sweet innocence in being human—in
not having to be just happy or just sad—in the nature of being
able to be both broken and whole, at the same time.*
—C. JoyBell C.

I wonder.

How many times do we grant ourselves permission to be human?

How many times do we simply allow ourselves not to be perfect?

Today, I wish for you your humanness.

Today, you get to stumble and fall and pick yourself back up again. You get to be human.

Today, you get to hurt and cry and learn to heal. You get to be human.

Today, you get to fall short and fail and try again. You get to be human.

Today, you get to feel lost and wonder and search for your answers. You get to be human.

Today, you get to stop and breathe and start again. You get to be human.

Today, you get to not prove anything to anyone. You get to be human.

Today, you get to be slowest and last and still know a victory. You get to be human.

Today, you get to simply be you and be completely okay with that. You get to be human.

Today. You get to be human.

October 13

Every time the song looped, all I heard was the part about the lies—and how they weigh you down. Tonight, as I drive toward Detroit in my Jeep, I know what those words really mean. It's not just the lies they're referring to. It's life. You can't run to another town, another place, another state. Whatever it is you're running from—it goes with you. It stays with you until you find out how to confront it.
—Colleen Hoover

There are times, I run from my pain

There are times, I run from my fears

There are times, I run from my failures

There are times, I run from my worries

There are times, I run from my emptiness

There are times, I run from my problems

There are times, I run from my demons

There are times, I run from my past

There are times, I simply stand, turn, and whisper, "Leave me alone."

October 14

The genius is he who sees what is not yet and causes it to come to be.
—Peter Nivio Zarlenga

I am not where I want to be.

I am not prepared for what awaits.

I am not strong enough.

I am not sure of all I can do.

I am not certain of the road.

I am not beyond my fears.

I am not equipped for the journey.

I am not ready.

Not yet.

Never underestimate the power of yet.

One simple word.

Yet, within it, are held all your answers.

October 15

A true love letter can produce a transformation in the other person,
and therefore in the world. But before it produces a transformation
in the other person, it has to produce a transformation within us.
Some letters may take the whole of our lifetime to write.
—Thich Nhat Hanh

This is a love letter. From you. To you.

Write your name on the two blank lines. Then quietly read it to yourself.

Dear _____,

I love you.

I love all the things about you that you wish were different.

I love your scars, for they show how you grew into a fighter.

I love your perceived imperfections, for they make you so real.

I love your story, for it speaks of how you became you.

I love all the things about you that you try so hard to hide.

I love your light, for no one else shines the brilliant colors of you.

I love your weaknesses, for within the fragile moments you have shown how strong
you truly are.

I love your wounded heart, for no matter how you are hurting, you are still a source of love.

I love all the things about you that you never want to speak of.

I love your gifts, for you have given so much, even when you believed you had nothing left to offer.

I love your magic, for you have shone through the darkness, risen from the falls, moved the mountain placed before you.

I love your beautiful, worthy, amazing self, for in all the world, no other was created to be simply you.

I love all the things about you. Unapologetically. Unconditionally. Unwaveringly. I love you.

Love, _____

October 16

Be where your feet are.
—Anonymous

I think that for much of my life, I have not been able to be where my feet are.

For replaying the past over and over and over in my mind. Somehow believing I could change an outcome, erase a memory, rewrite my history, or undo a mistake.

I think that for much of my life, I have not been able to be where my feet are.

For constantly looking ahead or worrying about what was yet to come. Somehow believing I should be further along my path. Or for spending time worrying about things I could not control.

I think that for much of my life, I have not been able to be where my feet are.

It applied to my running, as I was often not running the mile I was in. For looking ahead. For worrying about the looming hills. Fretting about the miles behind me.

It applied to my life, as I was often not living where my feet are. For looking at where I was not. For worrying about the future. Fretting about the past.

Today, I am right where my feet are.

Simply present and in the moment. There is no hurry or panic. No place I am rushing to be. Because I am supposed to be here.

Today, I am right where my feet are.

Simply present and in the moment. There is no doubt or worry. No need look behind me. Because I am supposed to be here.

Right where my feet are.

October 17

You do not have to know which path you must take. That's not how
life works. You simply must be curious and daring enough to take
a step into the unknown. That's how you come to know.
—*Toni Sorenson*

There are times I struggle.

So many places I want to be. So many directions I long to head. So many finish lines I seek to cross. And yet, I remain stationary.

Perhaps out of fear. Fear of not having answers. Fear of not knowing. Fear of failing.

Perhaps out of habit. I have walked the same path for so long. Why veer from it? I have found comfort where I stand. Why leave it?

Perhaps out of paralysis from analysis. For overthinking things. For the what-ifs. For the details and minutiae.

So, I do not move. And the longing aches remain. But they must be quelled. For I am restless.

And I come to realize, I do not need to overcome my fears, or have all the answers, or follow a detailed plan to get where I long to be.

I simply have to build the path.

This day, let me set forth to constructing my path. Toward my goal. In the direction I seek. To the dream I am dreaming.

October 18

All men dream: but not equally. Those who dream by night in the dusty recesses of
their minds wake up in the day to find it was vanity, but the dreamers of the day are
dangerous men, for they may act their dreams with open eyes, to make it possible.
—T. E. Lawrence

I once had a dream, and it frightened me.
For it asked more than I could give.
But when I opened my eyes, I was no longer afraid.
For I have so much more to give.

I once had a dream, and it frightened me.
For it was completely beyond my reach.
But when I opened my eyes, I was no longer afraid.
For if something is out of reach, I simply need move toward it.

I once had a dream, and it frightened me.
For I believed it would break me.
But when I opened my eyes, I was no longer afraid.
For I cannot be broken.

I once had a dream, and it frightened me.
For I thought I was not worthy of it.
But when I opened my eyes, I was no longer afraid.
For I have always been worthy.

October 19

I hope you do not let anyone else's expectations direct the course of your life.
—Julianne Donaldson

If I could just be me. I would run free.
For I would not be bound by expectations of another.

If I could just be me. I would shine.
For I would not be dulled by shadows cast by another.

If I could just be me. I would soar.
For I would not be caged by the fears of another.

If I could just be me. I would dance.
For I would not be paralyzed by the critiques of another.

If I could just be me. I would show you my magic.
For I would not be made invisible by another.

If I could just be me. I would be beautiful.
For I would not be the picture painted by another.

If I could just be me.

October 20

You are strong, tempered like steel in the fire and by the blows of the hammer of life. Nothing will break you again, only make you stronger and more whole. Perfection is the pride of those who have not lived, who know not these things in their arrogance. They remain the same—raw and without form. The hammer never touches them, and they lie on the shelf, gathering dust, slowly tarnishing and fading and crumbling. The blows of the hammer in the fire refine us into bright shining glory for the roles we play in life.
—Christina Engela

Steel (n.): modified form of iron having qualities of hardness, elasticity, and strength

Steel (v.): mentally prepare (oneself) to do or face something difficult

It is not that I am hardened as steel
It is that I refuse to be broken

It is not that I am tempered like steel
It is that I am able to withstand the heat

It is not that I am strong as steel
It is that I have learned to trust my strength

It is not that I am forged from steel
It is that I willingly accept the challenges before me

It is not that I am made of steel
It is that I do not fear the difficult.

October 21

When I dare to be powerful, to use my strength in the service of my
vision, then it becomes less and less important whether I am afraid.
—Audre Lorde

I can view myself as powerless. I cannot alter time. It passes. Inexorably. Moment by moment. Not slowed or advanced by my plans, goals, or dreams.

I can view myself as powerful. I can decide how I shall spend my time. It shall not be wasted or flittered away. I shall embrace the moments in pursuit of my dreams.

I can view myself as powerless. I cannot change another. Their choices. Their truths. Their path. These, theirs alone to own.

I can view myself as powerful. I can accept others as they come to me. Without judgment. Without prejudice. Without conditions. These, mine alone to own.

I can view myself as powerless. I cannot control outcomes. Stuff happens. Obstacles arrive. Uncertain is the future.

I can view myself as powerful. I can prepare for come what may. Whatever happens, I choose my response. Whatever the obstacle, I will be strong enough to overcome it. Whatever the future, I know I will be okay.

I am powerful when I simply choose to not view myself as powerless.

October 22

I come to you today with a smile.
Not for never having shed a tear.
But for knowing within every tear there was a great love.

I come to you today with a smile.
Not for never having been wounded.
But for knowing my scars are merely lines of my story.

I come to you today with a smile.
Not for never having sat with fear.
But for knowing fear could never stand up to my courage.

I come to you today with a smile.
Not for never having suffered defeat.
But for knowing I rose to my feet after every fall.

I come to you today with a smile.
Not for never having been broken.
But for knowing the best parts of me remained intact.

I come to you today with a smile.
Knowing smiles are contagious.
I hope this brings you a smile.

October 23

Acknowledging the good that you already have in your
life is the foundation for all abundance.
—*Eckhart Tolle*

I was given gifts,
But I shall never appreciate them
Until I choose to fully open them.

I was given freedom,
But I shall never embrace it
Until I loose the chains I alone have fashioned.

I was given faith,
But I shall never know its strength
Until I place the weight of my burdens upon it.

I was given hope,
But I shall never see its light
Until I dare wander away from the darkness.

I was given wings,
But I shall never soar to breathless heights
Until I learn to believe in them.

I was given love,
But I shall never feel the fullness of it in my heart
Until I accept my worthiness.

I was given this one beautiful life,
But I shall never come alive
Until I stand in wonder and gratitude for all I have been given.

October 24

You give but little when you give of your possessions. It is
when you give of yourself that you truly give.
—Kahlil Gibran

If I could offer a gift to you,
It would be the gift of my sight
So you could see without a filter
The beautiful light you cast upon me.

If I could offer a gift to you,
It would be the gift of my hand
So you could feel without trembling
The knowing of never having to walk alone.

If I could offer a gift to you,
It would be the gift of my words
So you could hear without discount
The truth of how amazing and special you are.

If I could offer a gift to you,
It would be the gift of my heart
So you could know without conditions
You are worthy of love.

If I could offer a gift to you,
It would not be of material things
So you could possess without debt
The best I am able to give.

October 25

In order to isolate what was possible, you had to
eliminate everything that was impossible.
—Jo Nesbø

The hard truth is that not everything you want, need, or desire is possible to achieve.

Despite what you may have been told or what you believe, some things are simply impossible. That is the bad news.

The good news? Once you understand and recognize what "impossibles" you are constantly trying to achieve, you can begin to make changes.

Changes that will ultimately lead to you successfully having all you want or need.

Here is what I call the "Impossible List":

1. Seeing the positive by always focusing on the negative

2. Building yourself up by constantly tearing yourself down

3. Making progress while making excuses

4. Becoming you by pretending to be someone or something you are not

5. Living and loving today by holding on to yesterday or worrying about tomorrow

6. Finding peace while holding on to regret, hurt, anger

7. Attaining happiness by waiting for someone else to be the source of it

8. Truly loving another without completely loving yourself

9. Having what you want while still believing you are not worthy

10. Achieving your dreams by simply hoping and wishing

I suspect there are more impossibles I could add to the list. And yet, for many of us, there is at least one item on this list for us to focus on.

And my wish for you is: now that you understand what is impossible, you will stop investing time and energy in those.

And that you begin to construct everything that is possible.

October 26

I hope you always knew.
—Aubrey Brewer

I did not get to say a last good-bye
Before you went away.
So for now, I shall simply whisper,
"We will meet again someday."

I did not get to say a last "I will miss you"
Before you went away.
So for now, I shall simply whisper,
"I will remember you all of my days."

I did not get to say a last "thank-you"
Before you went away.
So for now, I shall simply whisper,
"I can never repay my debt of gratitude."

I did not get to say a last "I'll be okay"
Before you went away.
So for now, I shall simply whisper,
"Your strength and faith will carry me."

I did not get to say a last "I love you"
Before you went away.
So for now, I shall simply whisper,
"I hope you always knew."

I did not get to see you
Before you went away.
So forever, I shall keep you with me.
Deep inside my heart.

October 27

I wondered what I could offer to you.

In hopes it would make a difference.

I offer to you my hope.

Please keep it close.

For within it, I have placed dreams, trust, faith.

I offer to you my light.

Please protect this flame.

For within it, I have placed courage, warmth, vision.

I offer to you my prayers.

Please hear them.

For within them, I have placed promise, healing, belief.

I offer to you my hand.

Please take hold of it.

For within it, I have placed strength, tenderness, the gift of friendship.

I offer to you my heart.

Please be gentle with it.

For within it, I have placed a story, a place called home, an unwavering love.

I wondered what I could offer to you.

In hopes it would make a difference.

And I came to realize, all I have to offer are simply pieces of me.

October 28

Only if you are possible, everything will be possible.
—Santosh Kalwar

I have nothing but this steady resolve
Ever willing to take one more step
Therefore, success remains possible.

I have nothing but this endless gratitude
Ever thankful for all my blessings
Therefore, happiness remains possible.

I have nothing but this constant belief
Ever trusting my wings are developing
Therefore, growth remains possible.

I have nothing but this quiet confidence
Ever humble yet aware of my gifts
Therefore, the dream remains possible.

I have nothing but this gentle heart
Ever following where it may lead
Therefore, love remains possible.

I have nothing but this unwavering hope
Ever believing in what is still unseen
Therefore, everything remains possible.

I have nothing, but I have everything.

October 29

I am thankful to God every day for the Gift of Life because even if I were the richest in the world, I still couldn't afford to buy Life.
—Gugu Mona

I was given a gift—
For the unwrapping,
Uniquely mine,
Priceless.

I was given a gift—
No instruction manual,
No return policy,
No exchange.

I was given a gift—
Irreplaceable,
Beautiful,
Fragile.

I was given a gift—
Presented with love,
Full of lessons,
For a reason.

I was given a gift—
May I always value it,
May I always treasure it,
May I always honor it.

I was given a gift.

I was given this life.

October 30

Joy is strength.
—*Mother Teresa*

Living is difficult

Difficult is continuing to believe

Continuing to believe is faith

Faith is trusting

Trusting is true courage

True courage is facing fears

Facing fears is growth

Growth is becoming you

Becoming you is happiness

Happiness is being grateful

Being grateful is giving unselfishly

Giving unselfishly is love

Love is joy

Joy is strength

For all things that lead you to joy require an act of strength.

October 31

Honor without power was a useless decoration and power
without honor was the simple flexing of muscle
—H. J. Brues

If you are going to flex...

Flex your smile. It is a brilliant light.

Flex your power to choose. Perhaps your greatest power of all.

Flex your right to remain silent. There is much to be learned by simply listening.

Flex your courage. Stop letting fear determine your decisions.

Flex your positive. You don't need to engage in the negative.

Flex your individuality. Be you. Always.

Flex your gratitude. Be thankful for the gifts, blessings, loves in your life.

Flex your beauty. Know it is not found in the mirror, but within you.

Flex your story. You can change the script you are writing, as you are its author.

Flex your love. Fill all the corners of your life with it.

November 1

Fear echoes your self-defined limitations, not your actual ones. To change your self-image, you must face what scares you.
—Vironika Tugaleva

I sat by myself. Believing I was alone. But all my fears were there to keep me company. Darkness. Silence. Loneliness. Failure.

I sat in the quiet. Believing I would hear nothingness. But all my fears spoke to me. Darkness. Silence. Loneliness. Failure.

I sat motionless. Believing I would feel the stillness. But all my fears made me tremble. Darkness. Silence. Loneliness. Failure.

By the dying embers of the fire, I invited my fears close. To come and sit with me. And one by one, they were addressed, unpacked, understood.

Darkness. I have always feared the darkness. For imagining the monsters that lurked there. For believing it to be the end of the light.

But as I sat in the darkness, I came to understand nothing exists there which lives in the light, and the dark must always yield to the light.

Silence. I have always feared silence. For it meant the echoes of my "I love you" had not been returned. For believing this silence spoke, "You are not worthy."

But as I sat in the silence, I came to understand if my "I love you" is not returned, it simply means I am worthy of so much more.

Loneliness. I have always feared the loneliness. For no one would be there to simply hold me in their arms. For no one would miss me when I was gone.

But as I sat with my loneliness, I came to understand taking comfort in the arms of another to not be alone is the truest loneliness. For being alone is not loneliness, but rather never learning to love one's self.

Failure. I have always feared failure. For it labeled me as not good enough. For it left so many dreams out of my reach.

But as I sat with my failure, I came to understand my life is not a contest. It is not to be judged based on what I attain or achieve, but rather, on whether I live with grace and love despite the heartaches.

I sat with my fears. Darkness. Silence. Loneliness. Failure. They exist. They are a part of me. They travel with me. But I came to understand, I no longer need to fear them.

November 2

Having a soft heart in a cruel world is courage, not weakness.
—Katherine Henson

For a child. For your child. For the child in you.

Dear Child,

It will not be easy living with a soft and tender heart. But you must remain courageous in the face of the hurt and ache you will encounter.

This type of heart is so very rare. Given only to those special angels who are strong enough to endure.

You have been given a gift. Precious and fragile. It will not be easy to care for it, as others will want to tarnish it, even break it.

Do not let them. Keep your heart soft.

Acting with kindness in a world filled with meanness is strength, not weakness.

Being soft-spoken in a world filled with noise is humility, not weakness.

Choosing to give in a world filled with takers is unselfishness, not weakness.

Offering peace in a world filled with violence is compassion, not weakness.

Believing in the good in a world filled with hatred is faith, not weakness.

Demonstrating understanding in a world filled with intolerance is love, not weakness.

Remember, sweet child, your heart was not filled with weakness. But rather, strength, unselfishness, compassion, understanding and goodness.

In a world filled with those who may not understand, be true to your heart.

Be kind. Remain humble. Act unselfishly. Walk in peace. Have faith. Spread love.

Love,

Me

November 3

Fear never scaled one mountain, never stepped up on a stage, never
accepted a challenge, never tilled new ground, never walked in a race;
he never even dared to dream. Fear failed to slay a single dragon.
Remember this before you choose to keep his company.
—Richelle E. Goodrich

This is your pep talk.

Have your fears
Have your doubts
Have your excuses
Have a way to rise above them

Have a goal
Have a vision
Have a dream
Have a plan to reach them

Have a letdown
Have a meltdown
Have a breakdown
Have a moment and get over it

Have a good day
Have a great day
Have a fabulous day
Have gratitude for having another day

Have faith
Have hope
Have belief
Have the courage to hold these always

Have a cause
Have a reason
Have a motivation
Have the discipline to live up to it

Have light
Have laughter
Have love
Have an understanding, these are a choice

You've just been pep-talked.

November 4

Your preparation for the real world is not in the answers you've learned, but in the questions you've learned how to ask yourself.
—Bill Watterson

Do I live the words I speak, or are they merely echoes of what I am too afraid to become?

Am I willing to cast aside the fears and doubts that reside in me, or do I allow them to continue to hold their spell over me?

Shall I move and grow and reach beyond this place of comfort, or shall I choose to build my stronghold here?

Will dreams I seek with eyes wide open be realized, or will I lie awake each night still holding them, wondering, "What if..."?

What shall be the anthem of my life, that I truly lived or that I could have?

It is such questions that launch me toward what I want my answers to be.

It is those answers that define who I want to be.

November 5

I will not try to convince you to love me, to respect me, to commit to me. I deserve better than that; I am better than that...Goodbye.
—Steve Maraboli

The loneliness came for knowing you were not alone.

The emptiness came for knowing was not my arms holding you.

The tears came for knowing you could not see what you did to me.

The sorrow came for knowing you turned away from the joy we knew.

The scars came for knowing how much your words now cut me.

The heartache came for knowing it was again my heart you played with.

For knowing. Came the good-bye.

November 6

Take the time today to love yourself. You deserve it.
—*Avina Celeste*

I took time to simply string the hours and days together.

I took time to simply unplug
To once again feel the electricity.

I took time to quiet the noise
To once again hear the laughter.

I took time to do nothing
To once again experience it all.

I took time to sit completely still
To once again feel myself falling.

I took time to close my eyes
To once again see a dream coming true.

I took time to let go the small things
To once again understand what matters.

I took time to stop being afraid
To once again trust this path.

I took time to simply lose myself
To finally find my everything.

November 7

Dear Friend,

I wish I could take your time
To give your weary some rest.

I wish I could take your pain
To give your heart some peace.

I wish I could take your darkness
To give your spirit some light.

I wish I could take your fear
To give your mind some freedom.

I wish I could take your burden
To give your steps some ease.

I wish I could take your worry
To give your hope some room to grow.

I wish I could take your doubt
To give your prayers some time to be answered.

I wish I could take your hand
To give your lonely some freedom to leave.

I wish I could take your heart
To give your life some unwavering love.

Love,

Me

November 8

Losing is an illusion that begins in your mind. Winning
is a certainty that ends in quitting.
—Nabil Basma

You can complain how hard it is.

You can fail to go the distance.

You can feel defeated.

You can line up all your excuses.

You can struggle, greatly.

You can fall short of the goal.

You can just not have it in you.

You can fall down repeatedly.

You can take a break.

You can whine and even cry.

You can lose your mojo.

But you can never, ever quit.

November 9

Sometimes the most scenic roads in life are the detours you didn't mean to take.
—Angela N. Blount

A man, a truck, an open road, a song, a whisper, a smile.

A man
Simple
Humble
Quiet
Gentle

A truck
Part machine
Part home
Headed to parts unknown
Headed toward a dream

An open road
Leading me forward
Leading me home
Calling my name
Calling my heart

A song
Familiar
The rhythm of my soul
Words I know by heart
Lyrics longing to be sung

A whisper
Barely audible
But my heart hears
It speaks of hope
It speaks my truths

A smile
For where I've been
For where I'm going
From a place of knowing
From a place in my heart.

November 10

Each patient carries his own doctor inside him.
—*Norman Cousins*

Here are twelve things to take for a healthier and happier you. Take as many as you need. Take them in abundance.

1. Take your time: Plan, prepare, allow for growth and mistakes, do the work, do not rush the process. This is true for just about anything of value that you seek.

2. Take compliments: You steal from the person who says something genuinely kind and honest about you when you deny his or her words. Accept them, as the gift they are intended to be.

3. Take feedback: You don't know everything. You never will. Be open to learning and growing and improving.

4. Take less than you give: Be a giver. Of compliments, of kindness, of forgiveness, of a hand, of yourself, of light, of love. Unconditionally. Unselfishly.

5. Take only what you earn: You are guaranteed nothing. Do not act as if something is owed you. If you want something, earn it.

6. Take nothing for granted: Not today, not your health, not friends or family; not this one, fragile, finite life.

7. Take time to just be: Relax, meditate, read, sit quietly, nap, breathe, slow down. Your body and mind and spirit will thank you.

8. Take little personally: It's not always about you. In fact, it rarely is. The meanness, pettiness, jealousy, anger, hatred, bitterness of others speaks of them, not of you.

9. Take responsibility: For your actions. For your words. For your choices. Place blame at the feet of no other.

10. Take ownership: Own your story. Own your signature. Own your gifts. Own your path. These belong solely to you.

11. Take the opportunities: To explore, to chase dreams, to smile, to create, to make a difference, to dance, to laugh, to see the world, to make magic, to feel goose bumps, to participate, to express gratitude, to fully live.

12. Take it one day at a time: Do not stress about what is yet to come. Be present. Focus on now. Much is lost for looking too far forward.

November 11

The things you do for yourself are gone when you are gone, but
the things you do for others remain as your legacy.
—*Kalu Ndukwe Kalu*

You inspire me
To write the words
To share my truths
To whisper from my heart

You inspire me
To try harder
To go farther
To reach higher

You inspire me
To seek the impossible
To rise from the struggles
To overcome the obstacles

You inspire me
To believe in me
To no longer doubt
To dream the dream

You inspire me
To choose discipline
To put aside my excuses
To be greater than my fears

You inspire me
To spread my wings
To move beyond comfort
To accept the challenges

You inspire me
To shine my light
To embrace my gifts
To try and make a difference

You inspire me.

November 12

No matter the situation, remind yourself, "I have a choice."
—Deepak Chopra

These, the choices I made this day.

I made the choice to believe in me.

I made the choice to walk a new path.

I made the choice to chase my dreams.

I made the choice to make today count.

I made the choice to be positive.

I made the choice to live in a way that honors me.

I made the choice to love where I am.

I made the choice to remind myself I have a choice.

November 13

Come tomorrow, I'll wake up new.
—Chad Sugg

This is another life chat.

Life: I have a gift for you.
Me: May I open it?

Life: Not yet, you must wait.
Me: Can you tell me about it?
Life: I cannot tell you.

Me: That seems unfair.
Life: It is a mystery to me as well.

Me: Well, how do you know it is a gift?
Life: Many others have asked for it.

Me: Does everyone get one?
Life: No. It is not granted to all.

Me: Is it valuable?
Life: You determine its worth. Many have let it go to waste. Others view it not as precious.

Me: I am confused. It doesn't sound as though I would want this.
Life: So, you do not want me to give you this gift?

Me: I am afraid. Can I return it if I do not end up liking it?
Life: I am sorry. It cannot be returned, nor can it be replaced.

Me: I have my doubts. I would prefer to know more.

Life: There is nothing more I can tell you. You must open the gift to see what it holds. So again, do you want my gift?

Me: I shall trust you. Despite my confusion, fear, doubt. I will accept your gift.

Life: This is good. My gift to you: tomorrow.

November 14

A child can teach an adult three things: To be happy for no reason, to always be curious, to fight tirelessly for something.
—Paulo Coelho

Lessons learned from eleven- and twelve-year-olds:

1. Friends matter.

2. Little things can hurt a whole lot.

3. It doesn't matter if you know how to dance, you should dance anyway.

4. When your inner child wants to play, let it.

5. No test can measure your awesome.

6. What you are looking for probably isn't in a textbook.

7. Members of the opposite sex are strange, scary, and oddly wonderful.

8. What is cool changes quickly.

9. If you don't know the lyrics, sing aloud anyway.

10. You might as well dream big.

If you pay attention, the little ones can teach you so much.

November 15

To follow, without halt, one aim: There's the secret to success.
—Anna Pavlova

I get asked frequently, "What's the secret?"

And I have come to the singular conclusion that no matter what they are asking the secret to (success, happiness, running faster, losing weight, living life), the answer is universal.

1. Fully commit to it: Not just part-time, not just when it feels good, or easy or convenient. Make it the way you go about business.

2. Believe in it: As though it is fact, as though it is the only option. So much that it becomes your signature.

3. Do not accept "no": Especially from yourself. Strike "I can't" from your vocabulary. Let "if only" never be spoken. I will. I will. I will.

4. Make no excuses: Accept none. Give none. Refute them. Do not succumb to them.

5. Trust yourself: Enough to know your worth. Enough to receive your gifts. Enough to make a statement of who you are.

6. Celebrate you: Find the joy. In the process, in the journey, in the doing.

But then again, I'm not telling you anything new. You've know this all along.

So in the end, I suspect, there is no secret.

November 16

Now I know what success is: living your truth, sharing it.
—Kamal Ravikant

I have no scientific research to back these claims.

I lack hard evidence to support these statements.

I cannot prove any of this beyond a shadow of a doubt.

And yet, there are just some things I simply know to be true.

These are ten truths about you.

1. You possess the capacity to succeed.

2. You are doing better than you ever give yourself credit for.

3. You are strong. Period.

4. You are not defined or confined by what others think.

5. You deserve to be happy.

6. You can choose to change your path.

7. You never need to apologize for being you.

8. You being you is the greatest gift you give yourself and others.

9. You have always been and always will be worthy of an amazing love.

10. You. Just you. More than enough.

November 17

Simply put: love does.
—Bob Goff

Love does not suck. Ever.
Love gently breathes color, life, hope into the empty pieces of you. Always.

Love does not leave. Ever.
Love remains through the trials, stumbles, difficult pieces of you. Always.

Love does not scar. Ever.
Love heals, soothes, stitches together the broken pieces of you. Always.

Love does not raise its voice. Ever.
Love softly whispers, quietly speaks amid the screaming pieces of you. Always.

Love does not rage. Ever.
Love calms, brings peace, adds serenity to the turbulent pieces of you. Always.

Love does not ghost. Ever.
Love stays close, remains visible, is a presence within the haunted pieces of you. Always.

Love does not judge. Ever.
Love welcomes, accepts, loves all the pieces of you. Always.

Love does not. If it does, it is not love.

November 18

The scars you were given
Do not mark you as a victim
They brand you as a warrior

The burdens you were given
Do not signal you as weak
They define you as a fighter

The trials you were given
Do not condemn you as a failure
They color you a work in progress

The brokenness you were given
Do not expose you as fragile
They shape you a gentle heart

The failures you were given
Do not label you as unworthy
They make you a human.

November 19

You'll see it when you believe it.
—Wayne Dyer

If you believe extending an act of kindness makes a difference, you can believe you are worthy of offering yourself the same.

If you believe gentle words are able to calm the fears of others, you can believe you have a voice within you to minimize all you are afraid of.

If you believe forgiveness frees one from the chains of bitterness and regret, you can believe it is okay to let yourself up from past mistakes.

If you believe in the existence of that which cannot be touched but is able to be held, such as hope and happiness, you can believe it simply waits for you to embrace it.

If you believe in another enough to give your heart away, you can believe in a love you have to give yourself.

If you believe in the sun rising tomorrow, you can believe in the miracle that is you.

If you believe. You can.

November 20

But regret is the thing we should fear most. Failure is an answer. Rejection is an answer. Regret is an eternal question you will never have the answer to.
—Trevor Noah

This is a story.

How do you handle rejection?
Of your ideas?
You continue to trust what you believe.
This is what is meant by faith.

How do you handle rejection?
Of your message?
You continue to speak your truth.
This is what is meant by honesty.

How do you handle rejection?
Of your dream?
You continue to seek your goose bumps.
This is what is meant by commitment.

How do you handle rejection?
Of your path?
You continue to walk with grace.
This is what is meant by humility.

How do you handle rejection?
Of your heart?
You continue to share your love.
This is what is meant by unconditional.

How do you handle rejection?

Of you?

You continue to make no excuses.

This is what is meant by integrity.

This is the moral of the story: It is not rejection that speaks of you. It is what you continue to do that speaks in greater volume about you.

November 21

Words! What power they hold. Once they have rooted in your psyche, it is difficult to escape them. Words can shape the future of a child and destroy the existence of an adult. Words are powerful. Be careful how you use them because once you have pronounced them, you cannot remove the scar they leave behind.
—*Vashti Quiroz-Vega*

This is a story.

Words
Express
Thoughts

Thoughts
Form
Intentions

Intentions
Lead to
Choices

Choices
Establish
Behavior

Behavior
Determines
Results

Results
Echo
Your words.

This is the moral of the story: Your words will come back to you. Choose those which speak of the results you seek.

November 22

If the only prayer you said was thank you that would be enough.
—Meister Eckhart

This is my only prayer.

Thank you for the struggles
For within, I have found my strength.

Thank you for the scars
For within, I have found my healing.

Thank you for the chaos
For within, I have found my blessings.

Thank you for the loneliness
For within, I have found my true self.

Thank you for the brokenness
For within, I have found my precious pieces.

Thank you for the silence
For within, I have found my voice.

Thank you for the darkness
For within, I have found my own light.

Thank you for the longing
For within, I have found my comfort.

Thank you for the failures
For within, I have found my will to try again.

Thank you for the lessons
For within, I have found my way.

Thank you.

This is my only prayer.

November 23

But...is simply the start of an excuse.
—Tony Garcia

This is your pep talk.

Get up
Get over it
Get moving

Your life
Your dream
Your choice

"But I can't" is a lie
"But I might fail" is fear speaking
"But" is simply the start of an excuse

Outlive your fears
Outrun your doubts
Outgrow your excuses

Of time, you are losing
Of action, you must take
Of yourself, you owe much

Your path is before you
Your next step to be taken
Your choice determines your fate

Life does not wait
Life no ifs, ands, or buts
Life has a message

Can you hear it?

Get your "but" out of your life.

You've just been pep-talked.

November 24

An excuse is the most expensive brand of self-defeat you will ever purchase.
—Johnnie Dent Jr.

Stop
Fearing
Worrying
Doubting

Stop
Waiting
Hesitating
Standing still

Stop
Crying
Whining
Complaining

Stop
Negating
Comparing
Discounting

Stop
Wasting time
Simply wishing
Making excuses

Stop
Looking back
Looking to others
Looking for the bad

Stop
Quitting
Stopping
Giving up

Just. Stop. It.

November 25

Go where your best prayers take you.
—Frederick Buechner

A prayer for you.

I pray for you a quiet
In which to hear your truth.

I pray for you a truth
In which your strength is spoken.

I pray for you a strength
In which you feel confident.

I pray for you a confidence
In which you come to finally believe.

I pray for you a belief
In which you can take comfort.

I pray for you a comfort
In which you find peace.

I pray for you a peace
In which you realize love.

I pray for you a love
In which you embrace yourself.

I pray for you.

November 26

Fear is a liar, it knows not your truth.
—Tony Garcia

Face what you fear
Embrace hope
Act with intention
Resolve to simply move forward

Insist upon discipline
Stay humble

At no point surrender

Let go what is not needed
Ignore the opinions
Answer to your heart
Respect yourself enough

Identify your non-negotiables
Trust your strength

Keep faith as your guide
Never settle for less
Own your story
Whisper "I can" again and again
Show up as you

No more excuses
Out with the negative
Trust more, worry less

You are worthy of your dreams
Operate from a place of belief
Unchain yourself, the lock is imaginary
Refute the impossible

Trade "I will" for "I did"
Respect the process
Untangle yourself from yesterday
Take no blessing for granted
Have your actions speak for you.

November 27

We are never truly loved, until we are loved for WHO and not WHAT we are.
—*Olaotan Fawehinmi*

I love you at times you know not.

I love you when you sleep
For it is then you find a peace I wish for you in my heart.

I love you when you wake
For it is then you greet the world with a beauty I see in my heart.

I love you when you feel unlovable
For it is then you will come to know you are ever worthy.

I love you when the world turns its back on you
For it is then you shall feel the presence of one always by your side.

I love you when the brokenness arrives
For it is then I wish to lie in your darkness, simply holding you in my arms.

I love you when your cupboards are barren
For it is then you shall realize it has always been just you, only you.

I love you when you do not love me
For it is then you may finally understand unconditional, unwavering love.

November 28

I love you with the words I left unsaid, with the silence
that I often spoke, that you still understood.
—Nessie Q.

"I love you" is echoed in every "I forgive you."
For love allows room for mistakes.

"I love you" is spoken in every "I am sorry."
For love accepts responsibility for its actions.

"I love you" is whispered in every "I believe in you."
For love sees what you cannot always know.

"I love you" is expressed in every "I am here for you."
For love places another as a priority.

"I love you" can be heard in every "I trust you."
For love does not fear being vulnerable.

"I love you" exists in every "I have no words."
For love does not clutter the space with noise.

In other words, I love you.

November 29

Time is a created thing. To say "I don't have time," is like saying, "I don't want to."
—Lao Tzu

This is a story.

If you have time to worry, you have time to trust.

If you have time to fear, you have time to find your courage.

If you have time to think of all the things that might go wrong, you have time to believe in what will go right.

If you have time to count your problems, you have time to add up your blessings.

If you have time to sweat the small stuff, you have time to figure out the stuff that truly matters.

If you have time to spend being angry, you have time to invest in being grateful.

If you have time to complain about someone, you have time to pray for them.

If you have time to doubt yourself, you have time to believe in yourself.

If you have time to sit and wish things were different, you have time to get up and make a change.

This is the moral of the story: You have time. It simply depends on what you choose to do with it.

November 30

Let it not be my words that speak of my strength.

But the silent simple act of rising to my feet once more.

Let it not be my words that speak of my commitment.

But the silent, simple act of showing up again today.

Let it not be my words that speak of my courage.

But the silent, simple act of taking the next step forward.

Let it not be my words that speak of my love.

But the silent, simple act of showing how much I care.

Let it not be my words that speak of who I am.

But the silent, simple act of remaining true to myself.

Let it not be my words that speak of my life.

But the silent, simple act of living.

December 1

I find the best way to love someone is not to change them, but instead, help them reveal the greatest version of themselves.
—Steve Maraboli

I did not come here to change your world.
But to change the way you view it.
For it contains beautiful hues of magic and hope and faith.

I did not come here to change your mind.
But to change the voice inside your head.
For you can, you will, you are.

I did not come here to change your path.
But to change the truth about where you are going.
For when you finally trust yourself, the next step becomes clear.

I did not come here to change your life.
But to change what you believe is possible for it.
For when you truly believe, anything is possible.

I did not come here to change who you are.
But to change how you see yourself.
For you are strong and beautiful and light.

I did not come here to change you.
But to love you.

December 2

Don't just love a person for the image, idea or concept of them, but love them for every fantastically weird and twisted detail that makes them up.
—Lauren Klarfeld

This. An open letter. Fill in your blank.

Dear _____ ,

I don't want just your beautiful.
I want your messy.
Your tired.
Your scars.

I don't want just your perfect.
I want your imperfections.
Your flaws.
Your chaos.

I don't want just your easy.
I want your "this is too hard."
Your burdens.
Your struggles.

I don't want just your "got it all together."
I want your disheveled.
Your untucked.
Your "I'm about to lose it."

I don't want just your calm.
I want your storms.
Your darkness.
Your turbulence.

I don't want just your pieces.
I want your everything.
Your wholeness.
Your all.

I want. Just you. For *this* is to love.

Love,

Me

December 3

*Remember you are capable of the most powerful thing
in the universe. You are capable of love.*
—AVA.

"What do you do when you want more than you are capable of?"

A friend posed this question, and it simply sat with me. I imagine many of us silently ask this question, in many phases of our lives. I know, as I have chased down some dreams, I faced my own version of this question. Perhaps, in the end, I do not have an answer, merely random thoughts. But here is where I landed.

1. Determine who or what has defined what you think you are capable of. Is it your past? Is it where you now stand? Is it previous attempts or failures?

That is often what we are led to believe. And, yet, it is false thinking. Your history does not pre-determine your future. Your current abilities are not your limit, but a place from which to grow. Failures are tools to guide you toward success.

2. Understand what has served as a barrier to a new level, to achieving a new goal, to reaching something currently beyond you. Do you have built-in defense mechanisms designed to keep you where you are—such as fear or excuses or patterns and habits you cling to?

This often requires us to truly examine our priorities, or day-to-day focus, and our willingness to do what is necessary to achieve more. Sometimes we won't like what we find. For it often calls into question our resolve, faith, discipline, desire.

3. Realize that any dream we hold or any goal we strive for should require us to grow into it. You see, the struggle itself, is the ultimate prize. For within is the strength and courage and fire that will lead you where you want to be.

This often means we must be willing to embrace the struggle, if we are to ever move beyond what we are presently capable of. It might require new, different, going beyond our comfort zone.

4. Get out of your head, get out of your way. Much of achieving what we want is determined by how much we truly believe we are capable, worthy, and ready to accept the dream. And much of what prevents us is our inability to get out of our own way.

This is often the hardest piece. Stop overthinking everything. Stop doubting yourself. Within you exists the power, strength, courage, and ability to alter your current reality. Oh, they may need to be tested and sharpened and fully developed, but they are in there. And this above all else, you must believe.

In the end, it can be summed up in three simple words: You are capable.

December 4

My mother was the most beautiful woman I ever saw. All I am I owe to my mother. I attribute my success in life to the moral, intellectual and physical education I received from her.
—George Washington

Lessons learned from my mom, through all the miles:

1. Be kind.
2. Be humble.
3. You are worthy.

4. Do your best.
5. Your best is enough.
6. You are enough.

7. You are loved.
8. Family first.
9. Tell the truth.

10. Use your manners.
11. Believe in yourself.
12. Give more than you take.

13. You can always come home.
14. It's okay to make mistakes.
15. When you are wrong, say, "I'm sorry."

16. You are not allowed to give up.
17. Miracles happen (you are a miracle).
18. You are never too old to listen to your mom.

19. Sometimes, bad things happen to good people. Be good anyway.

20. You are my legacy; honor yourself, and you honor me.

21. Even when I am not here, you are never alone.

For inside of you, I have placed my lessons, my memories, my love, my soul. I am always with you.

December 5

There's no giant step that does it, it's a lot of little steps.
—Peter A. Cohen

These. A series of little steps. That will get you there.

Step 1: Be willing to try.
For in the trying, you are actually doing. The victory is in the risk.

Step 2: Do not fear failing.
It isn't a state of emergency or a permanent state of being. Simply a chance to learn and grow and change.

Step 3: One step at a time.
Old news. Nothing new here. But in our constant state of "get there," we often skip important steps along the way.

Step 4: Focus forward.
You are less likely to stumble when walking forward. And where you are going isn't behind you.

Step 5: Each step is a first step.
So expect difficult. Expect it to take practice. Expect new. New fears, new challenges, new learnings.

Step 6: Remember, you are climbing.
It isn't supposed to be easy. It will challenge you. In the difficult, in the challenge, strength is developed.

Step 7: Stop doubting yourself.
For the last time and for your own sake, quit the negative self-talk. It doesn't look good on you. And, it doesn't help.

Step 8: Trust the ground.
Simple concept. If you feel afraid, take a knee. The ground is steady. And from there, you will again gain balance, courage, strength.

Step 9: Do not look so far ahead.
Stay where your feet are. It is the very next step, which is of most importance.

Step 10: Little steps are still steps.
Be patient with yourself. Be gentle upon yourself. Each new step, no matter how small, is still progress.

December 6

To be alone with yourself is to be alone. To be in the
company of others is to be alone together.
The only time you are not alone is when you forget yourself and reach
out in love—the lines of self blur, and just for a wild, flickering moment
you experience the miracle of other. And now you know the secret.
—Vera Nazarian

When you are lost inside, I will be there to find you.
I shall follow your trail of tears, for I know you are still hurting.

When you are lost inside, I will be there to find you.
I shall follow the words of your history, for they still speak of courage.

When you are lost inside, I will be there to find you.
I shall follow your light, for the darkness still cannot envelop it.

When you are lost inside, I will be there to find you.
I shall follow the sound of your heartbeat, for it is still beating strong.

When you are lost inside, I will be there to find you.
I shall follow your lifeline of hope, for it still remains unbroken.

When you are lost inside, I will be there to find you.
I shall follow your steps along this broken road, for you are still heading home.

When you feel lost inside, I will be there to find you.
And I shall simply remind you, "I've been here all along."

You may feel lost, but you are never alone.

December 7

We call a story about love a love story. We call a poem about love a love poem.
Well then, my dear, aren't our lives love lives?
—Kamand Kojouri

This is another life chat. Life knows.

Me: I did not go in search of love.
Life: And yet, somehow it found you.
Me: You know?
Life: I know.

Me: I did not think I was ready for love.
Life: And yet, somehow it arrived when you needed it most.
Me: You know?
Life: I know.

Me: I did not want to risk falling in love again.
Life: And yet, somehow it caught you.
Me: You know?
Life: I know.

Me: I did not know I could feel this way again.
Life: And yet, it is like nothing you have ever felt before.
Me: You know?
Life: I know.

Me: I did not know love filled so many missing pieces.
Life: And yet, it makes you feel complete.
Me: You know?
Life: I know.

Me: But how could you know so much about love?
Life: Dear child, love is what I am all about.

December 8

What we need is not the will to believe, but the wish to find out.
—William Wordsworth

For a child. For your children. For the child in you.

Dear Child,

As you stand before your challenge, I wish for you belief. A belief in your wings. You were made to soar. It is the reason you were gifted wings. Use them. Trust them.

But more than this, I wish for you a belief in your landing. You must always know you will land on your feet. Tall. Proud. Strong.

As you stand before your fear, I hope you can quiet the noise. You must drown out the voices wanting to speak of failing and "cannot."

But more than this, I hope you will listen for the whisper of your truth. You must always listen to the little voice daring to speak of "I can." "I will." For this is your story.

As you stand before your unknown, I pray you will let go. You must let go of the doubts and worries that, all too often, consume the air we breathe. Thus stealing our capacity to fully thrive.

But more than this, I pray you will hold on. You must always hold on to all that which allows you to breathe deeply. Hope. Faith. Love. For *this* is what allows us to fully live.

Love,

Me

December 9

*I have been driven many times upon my knees by the overwhelming
conviction that I had nowhere else to go. My own wisdom and
that of all about me seemed insufficient for that day.*
—Abraham Lincoln

This is my prayer. For you.

Dear Friend,

I know I am not there
Yet you are close in my heart
For you there is much care
As if we are not apart

I cannot erase the pain
Or ease the sorrow
I pray joy will remain
As you face tomorrow

May loving memories come to mind
For there, all of life is held within
May again a smile you find
And may healing now begin

I know not what you now face
And I cannot walk with you
But may you know God's grace
And feel a love so true.

Love,

Me

December 10

But some relationships aren't meant to last. They are worthy only till the time the two persons involved have time for each other. They do not know eternity. They live for the present, the now. And when distance plays it part, or life turns out to be busy, they fall apart. And maybe that's why they're never termed "Love." They simply remain what they were—mere "relationships."
—Sanhita Baruah

I thought you could love me forever
But you were too busy counting my years.

I thought you could love me completely
But you were too busy giving away pieces of yourself.

I thought you could love me without fear
But you were too busy being afraid of what others might think.

I thought you could love me without conditions
But you were too busy writing the rules.

I thought you could love me honestly
But you were too busy protecting your alibis.

I thought you could love me faithfully
But you were too busy cheating on yourself.

I thought you could love me simply
But you were too busy making it complicated.

I thought you could love me
But you were just too busy.

December 11

Our daily prayer ought to be: Please universe, help
me help myself and help me show others
how to help themselves.
—Kamand Kojouri

Please do not give up on me
I will get there
It is just my road has been so long

Please be gentle with me
I will get there
It is just my journey has made me weary

Please trust in me
I will get there
It is just my steps have been unsure and unsteady

Please believe in me
I will get there
It is just my path has been changed

Please be patient with me
I will get there
It is just my burden has been so very great

Please wait for me
I will get there
It is just I got a little lost along the way

Please keep loving me
I will get there
It is just my heart needed time to heal

Please. I will get there.

December 12

Sometimes you need to sit lonely on the floor in a quiet room in order
to hear your own voice and not let it drown in the noise of others.
—Charlotte Eriksson

I needed the quiet
To hear my voice
Whisper, "I am worthy."

I needed the quiet
To hear the echo of my strength
So I might rise again.

I needed the quiet
To hear my footsteps
Within each one taken, hope.

I needed the quiet
To hear my teardrops
Pain's cleansing bath.

I needed the quiet
To hear my answers
No longer questioning my truth.

I needed the quiet
To hear my silence
Drown out the noise.

I needed the quiet
To hear my heartbeat
To know I am not broken.

I needed the quiet.

December 13

Sometimes, reaching out and taking someone's hand is the beginning of a journey. At other times, it is allowing another to take yours.
—Vera Nazarian

Dear Friend,

Take my hand. Not so I may lead you or even to help you stand. Simply so you know you are not alone.

Take my light. Not so I may steer your course or light a single path. Simply so you know the darkness will not overtake you.

Take my time. Not so I may consume your moments or steal your day. Simply so you know, when you need me, I will be there.

Take my words. Not so I may speak for you or tell your truth. Simply so you hear a voice whispering, "I believe in you."

Take my heart. Not so I may take away your brokenness or replace the rhythm to which yours beats. Simply so you know a love unconditional.

Take my everything. Not so I may overwhelm who you are or take the place of anything. Simply so you know there is nothing you cannot ask of me.

This I offer you. Until you simply no longer need.

Love,

Me

December 14

If your actions don't live up to your words, you have nothing to say.
—DaShanne Stokes

If you forgive someone
Let "I forgive you" be more than spoken
Let it be the way you offer them unending grace

If you miss someone
Let "I miss you" be more than spoken
Let it be the way you carry yourself when they are away

If you are grateful for someone
Let "Thank you" be more than spoken
Let it be the way you always approach them

If you believe in someone
Let "I believe in you" be more than spoken
Let it be the way you faithfully stand by them

If you trust someone
Let "I trust you" be more than spoken
Let it be the way you simply open your heart to them

If you love someone
Let "I love you" be more than spoken
Let it be the way your heart holds them.

December 15

Sometimes, it's heavy. And you find a way to pick it up.

Sometimes, it's heavy. And you find a way to put it down.

Sometimes, you are weary. And you find a way to get it done.

Sometimes, you are weary. And you find a way to give yourself a break.

Sometimes, it's not enough. And you find a way to quiet the panic.

Sometimes, it's not enough. And you find a way to gently ask for more.

Sometimes, it's too much. And you find a way to surrender to it.

Sometimes, it's too much. And you find a way to make room for patience.

Sometimes, it doesn't make sense. And you find a way not to question it.

Sometimes, it doesn't make sense. And you find a way to let the answers unfurl.

Sometimes. You simply find a way.

December 16

Sometimes love doesn't look like what we think it should look like. Sometimes it's paradoxical. Sometimes we have to be more honest than we thought we'd ever have to be or more supportive than we are taught is appropriate. When we traverse those boundaries, that's when we really understand what this whole love thing is all about. We become more than just human. We become part of the giant, beautiful ever-changing reality of life. By loving without limits, we become wise, strong, and beautiful. We become more of what we already are.
—Vironika Tugaleva

Love. You are a paradox.

You take me places I have never been
Yet, you lead me home.

You fill me with pain
Yet, you are my very healing.

You cause the wall to rise before me
Yet, you show me the way through.

You push me to go faster
Yet, you are teaching me patience.

You leave me breathless
Yet, you breathe life into me.

You are always too much
Yet, you are never enough.

You are a complete unknown
Yet, you are an old friend.

You have me questioning myself
Yet, you help me find my answers.

You demand everything of me
Yet, you accept anything I have to give.

You make my heart race
Yet, you calm my trembling heart.

You are mine alone
Yet, I will never own you.

Love. You are a paradox.

December 17

So many believe that it is love that grows, but it is the knowing
that grows and love simply expands to contain it.
—William Paul Young

Love. I never knew.

I never knew you would become a part of my day. My life.

I never knew you would so often fill my thoughts. Now I cannot get you off my mind.

I never knew you would make me feel this way. Breathless. Alive. Complete.

I never knew you would be who I turn to. In times of need. In times of want.

I never knew you would captivate me so. Taking me completely in.

I never knew you would gently enter my dreams. Until you have become the dream.

I never knew you would make me fall in love. With you. With myself.

Love. I never knew. Now, you are all I know.

December 18

Grace is what picks me up and lifts my wings high above and I fly!
Grace always conquers! Be graceful in everything; in anger, in sadness,
in joy, in kindness, in unkindness, retain grace with you!
—C. JoyBell C.

The mistakes of this day
My clumsy attempts to grow
May I gently accept them
This, my act of grace

The scars I live with
Signals I have healed
May I no longer hide them
This, my act of grace

The tears still shed
Reminders of love known and lost
May I look back and smile
This, my act of grace

The stumbles ahead of me
When bowed and bent
May I seek strength in prayer
This, my act of grace

The fears I still know
Breathless on this ledge
May I simply exhale
This, my act of grace

My challenge
This and every day
Choose the path
That allows me to walk with grace.

December 19

I am a lover of words and tragically beautiful things, poor timing and longing, and all things with soul, and I wonder if that means I am entirely broken, or if those are the things that have been keeping me whole.
—Nicole Lyons

My struggle is not that I am lost
I simply wonder where I belong.

My struggle is not that I have doubts
I simply wonder what my truth is.

My struggle is not that I have fears
I simply wonder what I am so afraid of.

My struggle is not that I have known pain
I simply wonder why I insist on staying hurt.

My struggle is not that I have known failures
I simply wonder how long I will allow them to define me.

My struggle is not that I have no one to love me
I simply wonder when I will love myself.

December 20

Sometimes people don't understand the promises they're making
when they make them. But you keep the promise anyway. That's
what love is. Love is keeping the promise anyway.
—John Green

If ever I should find you.

I promise to give my time, my word, my hand, my heart, my love, my life.

I promise to kneel with you, stand by you, walk beside you, lay next to only you.

I promise "Good morning, beautiful" and "Good night, love."

I promise to listen to your dreams, to support you as you chase your dreams, to celebrate you as you realize your dreams.

I promise hugs in abundance, kisses in public, snuggles as needed, love as if it is endless.

I promise breakfast in bed, breakfast in Rome, breakfast by a campfire, breakfast without the cleanup.

I promise Christmas in July, Valentine's Day every day; you will be my favorite holiday.

I promise morning talks to evening walks.

I promise sunrises holding hands to moonlights holding you close.

I promise waking to dreams to falling asleep having lived a daydream.

I promise to do the work, to do my 100 percent, to do what I promised I would do.

I promise to grow with you, to grow old with you, to grow more in love with you.

I promise joy in the mundane moments, love in the difficult moments, life in the simple moments.

I promise joy without end, love without conditions, life without limits.

I promise you will know you are loved.

If ever I should find you. These are my promises.

December 21

All the trials we endure cannot be compared to these interior battles.
—Teresa of Ávila

I've been battling
An injury
An indifference
An inconsistency.

I've been battling
An I can't
An I don't care
An I don't want to.

I've been battling
My own inertia
My own inabilities
My own inadequacy.

I've been battling
My demons
My disappointment
My discontentment.

I've been battling
Old fears
Old habits
Old excuses.

I've been battling
New fears
New hurts
New struggles.

I've been battling
With failure
With myself
With change.

I've been battling
Without end
Without quit
Without surrender.

Bottom line: I've been battling.

December 22

The outer world is a reflection of the inner world. Other people's perception of you is a reflection of them; your response to them is an awareness of you.
—Roy T. Bennett

This is a story.

They said I was too old.

They said I was not good enough.

They said I was not worthy.

They said they could do better.

They said they did not want my gifts.

They said they did not need me.

They said I was not beautiful.

They said I did not believe in you.

They said I did not love you.

They. My fears. Kept me. From trying to love. From daring to fall. From risking it all.

They. My excuses. Kept me. From holding myself accountable. From living promises made to myself. From chasing my waking dreams.

They. My own words. Kept me. From having to be my own brand of special. From ever needing to be amazing. From the pressure of shining the beautiful light within me.

They. Your fears, excuses, and own words have defined your life. It is time to redefine how you shall live.

Courage must now be defined as no longer listening to your fears.

Strength must now be defined as possessing power to move beyond you excuses.

Love must now be defined as the art of simply allowing yourself to be you, without fear or excuse.

This is the moral of the story: What they say does not define you. Your definition is in your response.

December 23

Children see magic because they look for it.
—Christopher Moore

For a child. For your child. For the child in you.

Dear Child,

There is a magic in you, others may not believe. You see, this life has a way of making them think magic does not exist. But you are still powerful. For you can change the world. With a simple act of kindness. With a smile. With a helping hand. With a hug. With a "please" and "thank you." With a single choice to do good.

And never forget, someone thinks you are magical.

There is a light in you that others may not see. You see, this life has a way of making them focus on the darkness. But you must still beautifully shine. For your light can save the world. When you shine your light, you grant permission for everyone around you to shine their own. And when we all shine, there will finally be no more darkness.

And never forget, someone thinks you are beautiful.

There is a gift in you that others may not accept. You see, this life has a way of stealing gratitude from them. But you must still share your gift. For no one in the entire history of the world has ever been you. And we would be lesser for not having your gift. So sing your song. Dance your dance. Write your story. Leave your mark.

And never forget, to someone, you are a gift.

There is a dream in you, others may not understand. You see, this life has a way of making them believe dreams don't come true. But you must still dream, my child. For your dream is the dream the world has been waiting for. Dream big. Dream bold. Dream with your eyes wide open. Hold on to your dream. Dream every single day.

And never forget, you are someone's dream.

Love,

Me

December 24

At the end, one didn't remember life as a whole but as just a string of moments.
—David Levien

This is a story.

If you have but a moment
Go give someone a hug
As if for the first or last time
Just because you can

If you have but a moment
Kiss a loved one
As tenderly as only love can
Just because you can

If you have but a moment
Call an old friend
Simply to say, "I was thinking of you"
Just because you can

If you have but a moment
Express gratitude to someone
Simply for their presence
Just because you can

If you have but a moment
Choose words to begin healing
"I'm sorry" or "I forgive you"
Just because you can

If you have but a moment
Fill in someone's blank
"You are _____"
Just because you can

If you have but a moment
Let someone know you love them
Even if they are certain of this
Just because you can.

This is the moral of the story: Just because you can, is all the reason you will ever need.

December 25

And so this is Christmas.
—*John Lennon*

Dear Friends,

This is my wish for you this Christmas Day.

More than presents, may you be present.
May you remain present to the many blessings that fill your life.

More than gifts, may you be gifted.
May you be gifted peaceful and loving memories of the angels who once walked beside you.

More than wrapping, may you be wrapped up.
May the loving arms of family and friends enfold you, keeping you safe and warm.

More than lights, may you see the light.
May the light of a new dawn, a new hope, a new beginning, shine brightly upon you.

More than presents, gifts, wrapping, and lights...and so this is Christmas.

Love,

Me

December 26

The gift of life is so precious that we should feel an obligation
to pay back the universe for the gift of being alive.
—Ray Bradbury

There is a gift I received.
Once opened, all other gifts are made more valuable.
Gratitude.

There is a gift I received.
Once opened, it brought both laughter and tears.
Memories.

There is a gift I received.
Once opened, my gifts were multiplied.
Friendship.

There is a gift I received.
Once opened, it can never be returned or exchanged.
Time.

There is a gift I received.
Once opened, I am able to accept the gifts offered me.
Forgiveness.

There is a gift I received.
Once opened, fears of tomorrow no longer appeared.
Hope.

There is a gift I received.
Once opened, I no longer worry about gifts yet to arrive.
Faith.

There is a gift I received.
Once opened, I understood Christmas doesn't come but once a year.
Love.

There is a gift I received.
Once opened, I became joy itself.
Life.

Thank you for the gift you are in my life.

December 27

It's not what we do once in a while that shapes our lives. It's what we do consistently.
—Anthony Robbins

This is a story.

Consistency
Builds
Trust.

Trust
Fosters
Courage.

Courage
Instills
Hope.

Hope
Precedes
Faith.

Faith
Inspires
Dreams.

Dreams
Become
Possibilities.

Possibilities
Demand
Consistency.

This is the moral of the story: In the end, it is what we do with consistency that determines what is ultimately possible.

December 28

I know that the whole point—the only point—is to find the things that matter, and hold on to them, and fight for them, and refuse to let them go.
—Lauren Oliverto

For those of you fighting your way back.

This is for you.

I am fighting my way back
To a place of strength
Where I once again believe in me,
For *this* is to be strong.

I am fighting my way back
To a place of courage
Where I once again trust myself,
For *this* is to be brave.

I am fighting my way back
To a place of hope
Where I once again feel confident,
For *this* is to have faith.

I am fighting my way back
To a place of calm
Where I once again can exhale,
For *this* is to be at peace.

I am fighting my way back
To a place of no limits
Where I once again can grow,
For *this* is to know freedom.

I am fighting my way back
To a place of forgiveness
Where I once again let go,
For *this* is to live without regret.

I am fighting my way back
To a place of acceptance
Where I once again feel worthy,
For *this* is to be loved.

December 29

She who follows another's course, finds a sure path to her own remorse.
—John Kramer

This is your pep talk.

Open your cage.
Open your eyes.
Open your heart.
Close the negative.
Close the past.
Close the fear.

Pick up your chin.
Pick up your pace.
Pick up your self.
Drop the excuses.
Drop the guilt.
Drop the hammer.

Write a new verse.
Write a new chapter.
Write a new story.
Erase the doubt.
Erase the worry.
Erase the regret.

Listen to hope.
Listen to faith.
Listen to your voice.
Silence the noise.
Silence the critics.
Silence the nonsense.

Chase your dream.
Chase your goose bumps.
Chase your unicorn.
Follow no one.
Follow your path.
Follow your heart.

You've just been pep talked.

December 30

To be yourself in a world that is constantly trying to make
you something else is the greatest accomplishment.
—Ralph Waldo Emerson

This is a story.

It's not easy being me. Different.
In a world that values conformity,
I am often left standing alone.

It's not easy being me. Soft-spoken.
In a world that values noise,
I am often not heard.

It's not easy being me. Humble.
In a world that values pride,
I am often easily overlooked.

It's not easy being me. Sensitive.
In a world that values hardness,
I am often seen as weak.

It's not easy being me. Scarred.
In a world that values superficial,
I am often not seen as beautiful.

It's not easy being me. Unwavering.
In a world that values the fleeting,
I am often viewed as old-fashioned.

It's not easy being me. Committed.
In a world that values convenience,
I am often considered difficult.

It's not easy being me. Real.
In a world that values make believe,
I am often misunderstood.

This is the moral of the story: What comes with ease is often of less value. Be you.
Always.

December 31

They say to never look back. But sometimes I do.
It's gratifying to see how far I've come.
—Richelle E. Goodrich

This is an alphabetical retrospective.

Accomplished: Several dreams
Broken: Once again, this gentle heart
Conquered: Many fears

Danced: And oh, how I did dance
Enjoyed: All life has to offer
Fell: Deeply, completely in love

Goals: Reached a few, missed a few
Hoped: When nothing else was possible
Imagined: The impossible

Jumped: With both feet, without fear
Kissed: Every day, gently upon the lips
Loved: Unconditionally, unwaveringly

Mufasas: Felt the goose bumps
Never: Gave up
Opened: My arms, my heart

Prayed: For you
Quietly: Spoke my truths
Ran: Along a broken road

Simply: Loved. Lived
Traveled: In search of home
Understood: So much I still do not understand

Ventured: Beyond my comfort zone
Whispered: Truths from my heart
X marks the spot: Of places I'm still longing to go

Yearned: To be loved in return
Zero: Regrets

About the Author

Tony Garcia has learned a lot from being a father of four. The experience of fatherhood has shaped his twenty-seven-year career as a middle school teacher, his blossoming status as a motivational speaker and life coach, and his writing in ways that only a parent can understand.

While chronicling his journey to running the Boston Marathon, Garcia realized that he was writing about more than just running. He was conveying a message of hope, inspiration, and love that became his first book, *Wanna Know a Truth?* Since the publication of that book, Garcia has become a motivational speaker and shares his message with adults and children all across the United States.

In this follow-up volume, *Whispers from My Heart*, Garcia continues to document his personal journey toward enlightenment and realization.

73595820R00310

Made in the USA
Lexington, KY
11 December 2017